The Kids Book Of
CANADA

WRITTEN BY
Barbara Greenwood

ILLUSTRATED BY
Jock MacRae

KIDS CAN PRESS

For Bob, who is always willing to help me problem-solve and who has a gift for ferreting out the precise arcane detail I need

Acknowledgements

My thanks to Valerie Hussey and Ricky Englander for suggesting the subject and giving me the opportunity to tackle it. In a book crammed with multitudinous details, a writer needs the help of many keen minds and sharp eyes. My thanks to the whole Kids Can team for their help, particularly Marie Bartholomew for her book design and Jock MacRae for giving shape and colour to the text with his illustrations. Special thanks to Liz MacLeod, my editor, for her painstaking reading of the manuscript and expert help in checking elusive details.

We acknowledge the support of the Canada Council for the Arts
and the Ontario Arts Council for our publishing program.

Canadian Cataloguing in Publication Data

Greenwood, Barbara [date]
The kids book of Canada: exploring the land and its people
Includes bibliographical references.
ISBN 1-55074-315-5

1. Canada — History — Juvenile literature.
2. Canada — Geography — Juvenile literature.
I. MacRae, Jock. II. Title.

FC58.G73 1997   j971   C97-930195-5
F1008.2.G73 1997

First U.S. Edition 1998

Text copyright © 1997 by Barbara Greenwood
Illustrations copyright © 1997 by Jock MacRae

Flags and coats of arms are from the book *Symbols of Canada*.

Flags and coats of arms are reproduced with the kind permission of: the Department of Canadian Heritage; Protocol and Events Branch, British Columbia Ministry of Government Services; The Government of Alberta; Saskatchewan Provincial Secretary; Manitoba Culture, Heritage and Citizenship; Ontario Government; ministère de la Justice du Québec; Intergovernmental Affairs, New Brunswick; Nova Scotia Department of Supply and Services; Executive Council Office, Province of Prince Edward Island; Government of Newfoundland and Labrador; Government of the Northwest Territories; The Government of Yukon. The coat of arms symbol of the Province of Ontario is protected by law and is reproduced here with permission.

Population figures throughout this book are from the Statistics Canada 1996 census.

Published in Canada by: Published in the U.S. by:
Kids Can Press Ltd.   Kids Can Press Ltd.
29 Birch Avenue   85 River Rock Drive, Suite 202
Toronto, ON M4V 1E2   Buffalo, NY 14207

Edited by Elizabeth MacLeod
Designed by Marie Bartholomew
Printed in Hong Kong by
Wing King Tong Co. Ltd.

CM 97 0 9 8 7 6 5 4 3 2

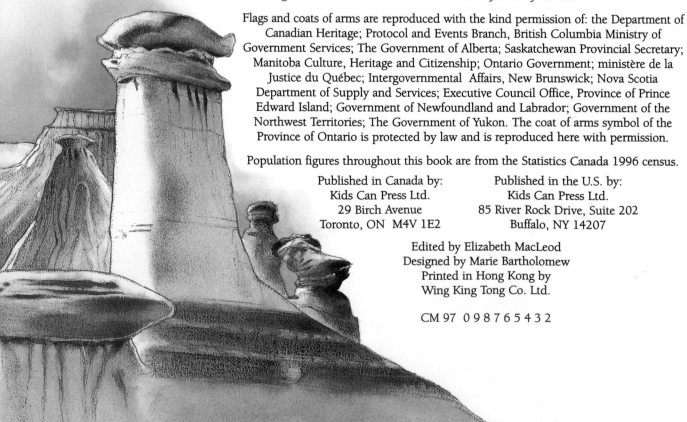

CONTENTS

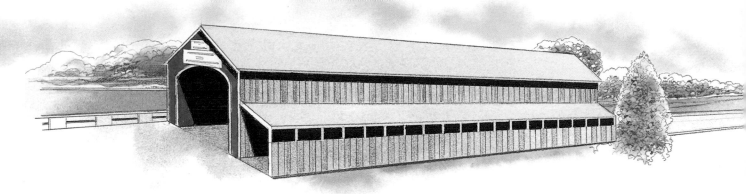

CANADA

Canada's name comes from the Huron-Iroquois word *kanata*, meaning "village." The French explorer Jacques Cartier first used it in 1535 to describe a small area on the St. Lawrence River. Now it refers to the world's second-largest country. Canada stretches 5513 km (3426 mi.) from the Atlantic Ocean to the Pacific Ocean, and 4634 km (2880 mi.) from the United States border almost to the North Pole. The ten provinces and two territories represent a great variety of landscapes — from mountains to plains, forests to grasslands, and waterfalls to badlands. Forestry and mining are important northern industries, while crops such as wheat, apples and potatoes are grown in the south. Fishing was once the biggest coastal industry. Canada's people come from many different backgrounds and traditions. The majority of the people live in large cities near the southern border.

Quick facts

Population: 28 846 761

Size: 9 970 610 km^2
(3 849 953 sq. mi.)

Capital: Ottawa, Ontario
(pop. 763 426)

Other major cities:

Toronto, Ontario
(pop. 4 263 757)

Montreal, Quebec
(pop. 3 326 510)

Vancouver, British Columbia
(pop. 1 831 665)

Main industries: agriculture, mining, forestry

Official languages: English and French

National anthem: "O Canada"

Coat of arms

Canada's earliest European settlers are represented by the three royal lions of England, the royal lion of Scotland, Ireland's harp and France's fleur-de-lis. The maple leaves represent Canada's forests. The lion of England holds the British flag and the unicorn of Scotland holds the flag of Royal France. Below are the French fleur-de-lis, the Irish shamrock, the Scottish thistle and the English rose.

Motto

A MARI USQUE AD MARE
(From sea to sea)

Flag

Canada's official colours, red and white, come from England's cross of St. George. The maple leaf has been a symbol of Canada since the early French settlements. The flag first flew on February 15, 1965.

Animal

Canada's first important industry, the fur trade, was based on the beaver.

4 Taiga landscape is a mixture of swampy areas of dwarf birch and willow, and drier areas of small trees such as trembling aspen and black spruce.

3 Tundra is low, flat land covered with lichens, mosses and small shrubs. The climate is cold and dry.

The group of islands at the top of Canada is known as the Arctic Archipelago. It is covered with ice and snow for ten months of the year.

The Canadian Shield, a rocky area surrounding Hudson Bay, is covered by lakes and forest. Gold, silver, copper and nickel are mined from the rock.

5 The Boreal Forest, a wide band of evergreen trees, stretches across most of the provinces.

7 The Hudson Bay Lowland, a marshy area, is home to many waterfowl.

ARCTIC OCEAN

HUDSON BAY

ATLANTIC OCEAN

UNITED STATES OF AMERICA

MONTREAL

OTTAWA

TORONTO

THE GREAT LAKES

1 The Pacific Coast is an area of rainforests.

2 The Western Cordillera is made up of several mountain ranges.

6 The Interior Plains, or prairies, are the remains of ancient seabeds.

9 The Mixed Wood Forest contains maple, oak and walnut trees.

8 The mountains of the Appalachian Region have been worn down by erosion. Good farmland is found in the valleys.

PEOPLE, PLACES AND EVENTS

On November 7, 1885, at Craigellachie, British Columbia, the last spike was driven to complete the Canadian Pacific Railway and link Canada from west to east.

Long ago, every town operated on different times. This was confusing for railroads, so railway builder Sanford Fleming suggested the world be divided into 24 time zones, each one differing by an hour from the next. His idea, called Standard Time, was adopted around the world on January 1, 1885. Now, when it is noon in Ottawa, it is always 1:00 P.M. in Halifax and 9:00 A.M. in Vancouver.

Canada is known as the country north of the 49th parallel of latitude. This line was chosen in 1818 as the border across the prairies from the Great Lakes to the Rockies because there were no natural landmarks that could be used to mark the division between Canada and the United States.

HISTORY OF THE COUNTRY

Canada's earliest settlers likely came across the Bering Strait from Asia about 12 000 years ago. They spread across the continent developing different traditions. The first Europeans to see North America were probably sailors. Soon fishing fleets from Spain, Portugal and England were coming to the Grand Banks.

1608

France sent explorers, including Samuel de Champlain, to the east coast and St. Lawrence River. In 1608 a colony, New France, started near modern-day Montreal. Later, Acadia developed in what are now the Maritime provinces.

1713

When France was defeated in war in 1713, its colonies in Canada became British. At first the French were allowed to keep their farms, but as more British settlers arrived there were quarrels over land. By 1755 Acadian farmers were forced off their land and sent to France and the American colonies. As more British settlers arrived, New Brunswick was created from part of Nova Scotia, and in 1791 Quebec was divided into Upper Canada and Lower Canada.

Among the many inventions Canada has given to the world is the Canadarm, an electrically operated, mechanical arm that can be mounted on the side of a space shuttle. It is 15.2 m (50 ft.) long, has helped repair satellites and soon will help build a space station.

In 1962 Canada became the third country to design and build a satellite when *Alouette I* was launched.

The Trans-Canada Highway runs 7777 km (4833 mi.) across Canada from St. John's, Newfoundland, to Victoria, British Columbia. It was completed in 1962.

In 1936 the Canadian Broadcasting Corporation (CBC) was formed to help all sections of this vast country keep in touch. Today the CBC broadcasts in French and English and beams programs in Aboriginal languages to the Arctic by satellite.

1812

In 1812 the United States declared war on the British colonies. The colonies had few settlers but they managed to stop the invaders. After the war, the people began to demand the right to make their own laws. When Britain refused, rebellion broke out in Upper and Lower Canada in 1837. Although the rebels were defeated, by 1841 the laws were changed to allow settlers to vote on local matters.

1867

Canada East and Canada West (formerly Upper and Lower Canada) joined with Nova Scotia and New Brunswick to form one country in 1867. In 1870 Canada acquired Rupert's Land around Hudson Bay, as well as the Northwest. British Columbia joined in 1871 and Prince Edward Island in 1873. By 1912, Manitoba, Alberta, Saskatchewan, the Yukon and the Northwest Territories were the size and shape they are today.

RUPERT'S LAND

1930s

Canada prospered until the 1930s when a worldwide depression left many people unemployed. After World War II (1939–45) Canada was thriving again and many immigrants arrived. Newfoundland became a province in 1949. Although Canada was an independent country, the British Parliament still had to approve all its laws. The Constitution Act of 1982 made the Canadian Parliament responsible for passing laws.

TODAY

As well as seeking more markets for its goods, a changing Canada is working towards new provincial roles in Confederation.

BRITISH COLUMBIA

British Columbia, Canada's third-largest province, was named by Britain's Queen Victoria. This mountainous province has three mountain ranges that run north-south. Between the ranges, a plateau provides grassland for cattle ranching. River valleys, especially the Okanagan Valley, shelter orchards of fruit such as peaches and apples. Heavy rainfall and mild temperatures along the coast create good growing conditions for flower gardens as well as food crops. Most of the population lives in the southwest corner of the province, particularly around the city of Vancouver. A chain of islands, starting with the largest, Vancouver Island, protects the coast from storms. The islands and coast are covered with stands of giant Douglas spruce and red cedars, making forestry a major industry. Fishing and mining are also important.

Motto

SPLENDOR SINE OCCASU
(Splendour without diminishment)

Quick facts

Population: 3 724 500

*Size: 947 800 km^2
(365 975 sq. mi.)*

*Capital city: Victoria
(pop. 304 287)*

*Other major cities:
Vancouver (pop. 1 831 665)
Nanaimo (pop. 85 585)
Prince George (pop. 75 150)*

Main industries: forestry, mining, agriculture, fishing

*Entered Confederation:
July 20, 1871*

Coat of arms

The British flag at the top of the shield shows the province's beginnings as a British colony. The blue bars represent the Pacific Ocean, and the setting sun shows the province's westerly position in Canada. The coat of arms also features a wapiti, a bighorn sheep and dogwood flowers.

Flag

The design is taken from the shield.

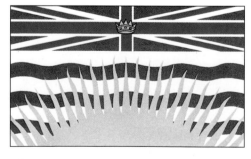

Flower

The Pacific Dogwood is covered with white blossoms in spring and bright red berries in the autumn.

Bird

Stellar's Jay is found in the Pacific rainforest.

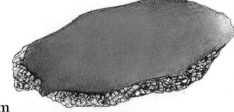

Tree

The Western Red Cedar often reaches heights of 60 m (197 ft.), three times that of the average White Cedar.

Gem

Jade, used in jewellery and for sculptures, is found in many shades of green.

Pacific salmon swim up the Fraser, Skeena and other coastal rivers to spawn (lay their eggs). Many are caught in nets and shipped to canning factories.

The Peace River Lowlands contain deposits of petroleum, natural gas and coal. Wheat is also grown here.

Orcas (killer whales), seals, sea otters and sea lions as well as many varieties of sea birds live along the Pacific coastline.

A forested mountain area, the Boreal Cordillera is home to moose, grizzly bears and mountain sheep.

The Montane Cordillera is a mountainous area with a dry climate. The northern section has trees but the south is desert-like. The Boreal Plains are covered with muskeg, ponds, and forests of small trees.

Fjords are long, narrow inlets of the sea that glaciers cut out of the coastal cliffs.

The rolling, hilly country of the Interior Plateau is used for cattle ranching.

The Pacific Coast was once covered by thick forests of gigantic spruce and cedar.

The Rocky Mountain Trench runs along the west side of the mountain range. The Columbia, Kootenay, Fraser and other rivers flow out of this long valley.

British Columbia's three major mountain ranges are the Coast Mountains, the Columbia Mountains and the Rocky Mountains.

Mount Robson, which rises to 3954 m (13 000 ft.), is the highest peak in the Rocky Mountains.

The Okanagan Valley produces apples, apricots, cherries, peaches, pears and plums on its dry, sunny slopes.

QUEEN CHARLOTTE ISLANDS

Skeena R.

Peace R.

Rocky Mountains

PRINCE GEORGE

Fraser R.

Columbia Mountains

MT. ROBSON

Coast Mountains

VANCOUVER ISLAND

NANAIMO

VANCOUVER

OKANAGAN VALLEY

Columbia R.

Kootenay R.

PACIFIC OCEAN

VICTORIA

PEOPLE, PLACES AND EVENTS

At Barkerville, a restored gold-rush town, visitors can pan for gold just as the early prospectors did.

Emily Carr (1871–1945) was one of the first artists to paint the life of the West Coast Aboriginal people.

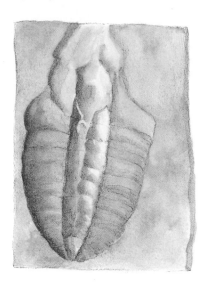

Terry Fox (1958–81), who lost most of one leg to cancer, inspired everyone with his incredible courage as he raised money for cancer research by running across Canada. He died in New Westminster in June 1981.

In Yoho National Park a rock formation called the Burgess Shale contains preserved fossil remains of nearly 140 species of prehistoric creatures, such as sea worms, sponges and trilobites.

HISTORY OF THE PROVINCE

Among the original Aboriginal Nations of the coast are the Haida, Nootka, Bella Coola, Tlingit and Salish. For thousands of years they have lived in the Pacific area, fishing for salmon and seals and hunting deer, elk and mountain goats. Many are skilled at woodworking, building large plank houses and carving totem poles.

JAMES COOK

1770s

During the 1770s Spain and Russia wanted the north Pacific coast, but Britain claimed it first. In 1778 Captain James Cook charted part of the coast. Later George Vancouver mapped more than 16 000 km (9940 mi.) of coastline. In 1793 Alexander Mackenzie travelled overland to the Pacific Ocean. As a result of these efforts, Vancouver Island and the coastal area became British.

1805

Europeans began setting up fur-trading posts along the coast and main river routes in 1805. They also brought guns and diseases that weakened Aboriginal society. In 1846, when American settlers moved into the Pacific coast, the area was divided and Vancouver Island and the mainland north of the 49th parallel became a British colony.

Families of orcas, or killer whales, can be seen off the Pacific coast as they migrate.

The first roll of newsprint manufactured in western Canada was produced in Powell River in 1912.

A monster called Ogopogo is said to live in Lake Okanagan. Although many people claim to have seen it, no one has ever caught it. Try saying its name backwards.

Poet and actor Chief Dan George (1891–1981) of the Squamish Band recited his "Lament," a poem about Aboriginal defeat and revival, at the Canadian Centennial celebrations in Vancouver in 1967.

In 1993 Kim Campbell became Canada's first female prime minister. She was born in Port Alberni.

1857

When gold was discovered in the Fraser River Valley (1857) and in the Cariboo Mountains (1860), thousands of prospectors flocked in. The area was declared a British colony. In 1866 the Interior joined with the coastal colony to become British Columbia.

1871

In 1871 British Columbia joined Confederation after Canada promised to build a railway to link the province with the rest of the country. In the 1880s thousands of Chinese labourers arrived to work on the railway. Some stayed on after it was finished in 1885. In the 1890s Japanese immigrants came to work at fishing and market gardening. The railway brought many British settlers from the east. By 1900 Vancouver was bustling.

1900s

By the early 1900s natural products, such as coal, gold, copper and lumber, were making British Columbia wealthy. But the Great Depression of the 1930s brought unemployment. It wasn't until after World War II (1939–45) that projects such as hydroelectric dams and the aluminium smelter at Kitimat created new jobs.

TODAY

Immigration is bringing many new citizens to British Columbia. As the population grows, the province is more and more concerned about maintaining its rainforests and other natural resources.

ALBERTA

Alberta was named for Queen Victoria's fourth daughter, Princess Louise Caroline Alberta, and is the most westerly of the Prairie provinces. The rolling foothills of southern Alberta make excellent ranch country and the grasslands are good for growing wheat. Farther north the province is covered by forests of spruce and pine, with many glacier-fed rivers and lakes. Such cold winters follow the warm summers that southern Albertans look forward to chinooks, the warming winds that blow out of the mountains in late January. Settled by people of many heritages, the province was first known for wheat and cattle production. From the 1950s to the 1980s, oil discoveries made it rich. Today the manufacturing of oil products, plastics, forest products and computers is also important.

Motto

FORTIS ET LIBER
(Strong and free)

Quick facts

Population: 2 696 826

Size: 661 190 km² (255 305 sq. mi.)

Capital city: Edmonton (pop. 862 597)

Other major cities: Calgary (pop. 821 628) Lethbridge (pop. 63 053) Red Deer (pop. 60 075)

Main industries: oil production, mining, agriculture, cattle ranching

Entered Confederation: September 1, 1905

Coat of arms
The top of the shield shows the cross of St. George, patron saint of England. The lower section represents Alberta's landscape: mountains, foothills, prairie and grain fields. Around the shield are a beaver, a lion, a pronghorn and wild roses.

Flag
The flag has the provincial shield centred on a background of royal blue, one of Alberta's official colours.

Flower
The Wild Rose produces scarlet berries that are used as winter food by birds.

Bird
The Great Horned Owl hunts ducks, rabbits and other small animals at night.

Animal
Rocky Mountain Big Horn Sheep range over the upper slopes of the mountains.

Tree
Poles made from the Lodgepole Pine were used by Plains Nations to support their tipis.

Stone
Petrified wood is plant matter that has been turned to stone as minerals dissolved in water gradually fill the plant cells.

The Boreal Forest of pine and spruce covers most of northern Alberta. It provides homes for such animals as elk, grizzly bear and beaver.

The northern Taiga Plains are lowlands of marshes and swamps with permafrost underneath. Few trees grow here.

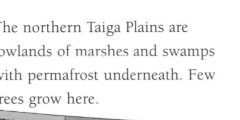

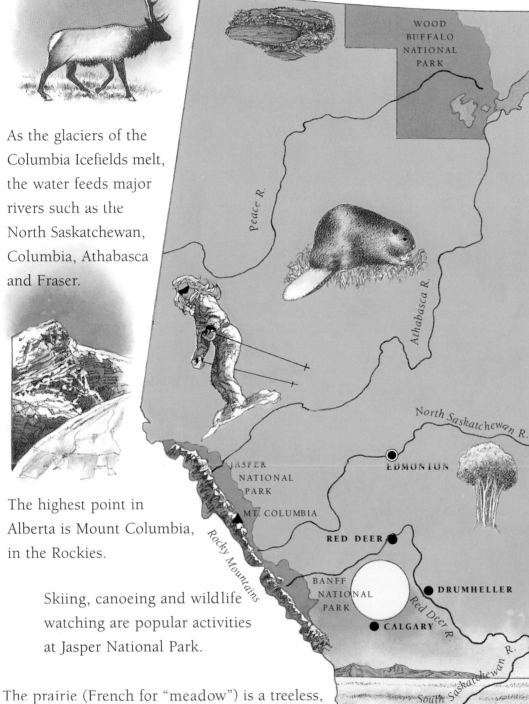

The Aspen Parkland has rolling hills, good soil and enough rainfall to grow crops. Its name comes from the groves of trembling aspen trees that grow here.

As the glaciers of the Columbia Icefields melt, the water feeds major rivers such as the North Saskatchewan, Columbia, Athabasca and Fraser.

At Drumheller, nearly 500 dinosaur skeletons have been discovered in the rocky shale. One was the flesh-eating *Albertosaurus*.

The highest point in Alberta is Mount Columbia, in the Rockies.

Skiing, canoeing and wildlife watching are popular activities at Jasper National Park.

The prairie (French for "meadow") is a treeless, grassy plain. It was once an ancient seabed. Now it is used for growing wheat.

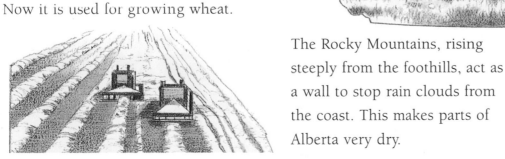

The Rocky Mountains, rising steeply from the foothills, act as a wall to stop rain clouds from the coast. This makes parts of Alberta very dry.

In the desertlike badlands, the Red Deer River has worn away the soft rock, leaving bluffs, gullies, and rock towers called hoodoos.

13

PEOPLE, PLACES AND EVENTS

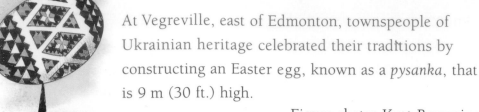

At Vegreville, east of Edmonton, townspeople of Ukrainian heritage celebrated their traditions by constructing an Easter egg, known as a *pysanka*, that is 9 m (30 ft.) high.

Horses weren't used by the Aboriginal people of Alberta or the rest of the prairies until after 1730 when herds set loose by Spanish explorers migrated north from Mexico.

Figure skater Kurt Browning, born in the foothills town of Caroline, has won four World and four Canadian Championships.

Before the coming of the horse, Plains Nations hunted by driving bison over cliffs at places such as Head-Smashed-In-Buffalo-Jump.

HISTORY OF THE PROVINCE

Aboriginal people have lived in the area now called Alberta for thousands of years. In the north, they hunted moose and deer and gathered wild plants and berries. On the plains they followed the herds of bison (buffalo), using their hides to make tipis and drying their meat to make pemmican.

1754

Europeans began exploring the area in 1754, and soon fur traders were building trading posts along the rivers. Fort Edmonton on the Saskatchewan River later became the site of the capital city. In the early 1800s explorer David Thompson made the first maps of the area.

1870

To encourage settlement, in 1870 Britain cancelled the Hudson's Bay Company's licence to trade in the Northwest and gave the vast area to Canada. The North-West Mounted Police opened a post at Fort

Macleod to keep law and order. Most Aboriginal people were soon moved to reserves, and the bison, which they hunted for food, were almost wiped out by European hunters.

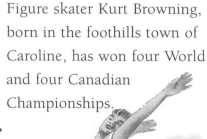

The whooping crane was once nearly extinct. Now, although it is still an endangered species, about 160 adult birds nest in the wetlands of Wood Buffalo National Park.

In 1916 Emily Murphy (1868–1933) became the first woman magistrate in the British Empire. In 1929 she helped win a fight to prove that women were legally "persons" and could therefore sit in the Senate.

The Calgary Stampede, started in 1912, is a ten-day celebration of the rodeo skills, such as bronc riding, steer wrestling and calf roping, that cowboys needed in early ranching days and still use today.

1897

In 1897, government advertisements in countries such as Hungary, Russia and Ukraine attracted thousands of immigrants. They travelled west on the Canadian Pacific Railway to farm the prairies. Because there were few trees, they spent their early years in huts built from sods (squares of earth and grass cut from the prairie).

1930

The Great Depression hit Alberta very hard, especially when world prices for wheat and beef dropped. Many Albertans raised cattle and grew wheat for export so when prices paid for both fell, the farmers had no money. Then came years of drought. Many people were forced to leave their farms.

1947

In 1947 oil was discovered at Leduc, south of Edmonton. This oilfield and others found over the next 30 years made Alberta wealthy. Jobs were plentiful in the oil industry, and Edmonton and Calgary grew into large centres.

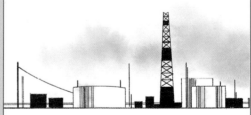

TODAY

In the late 1980s oil prices fell and companies couldn't afford to employ so many people. Since then the Alberta government has had to make many cuts to its budget.

SASKATCHEWAN

Saskatchewan's name comes from a Cree word meaning "swift-flowing river," and was first given to the mighty river that flows, in two branches, through the central part of the province. The middle Prairie province, located between Manitoba and Alberta, Saskatchewan is known worldwide for its production of wheat. More than one-third of its people live on farms. The rest live in towns and cities, and most live in the two biggest cities, Saskatoon and Regina. The capital of the province, Regina, was once known as Pile O' Bones because Aboriginal people cleaned buffalo hides and dried meat there. Later the name Regina (the Latin word for "queen") was chosen to honour Queen Victoria. Saskatchewan's climate alternates between scorching summers and frigid winters with frequent blizzards. Winds blow almost constantly over the flat grasslands of the south.

Motto
MULTIS E GENTIBUS VIRES
(From many peoples strength)

Quick facts

Population: 990 237

Size: 652 330 km^2
(251 884 sq. mi.)

Capital city: Regina
(pop. 193 652)

Other major cities:
Saskatoon (pop. 219 056)
Prince Albert (pop. 41 706)
Moose Jaw (pop. 34 829)

Main industries: agriculture, mining, petroleum refining

Entered Confederation:
September 1, 1905

Coat of arms
The red lion represents England. The three sheaves of wheat show the province's chief product. On either side of the shield are a royal lion and a white-tailed deer, both wearing bead work crafted by Aboriginal people of the Prairies.

Flag
The green section represents forest land, and the gold section, grain fields. The provincial shield is in the top left corner and the Western Red Lily is on the right.

Flower
The Western Red Lily grows in marshy meadows.

Bird
Sharp-tailed Grouse live on the ground and are often hunted as game.

Tree
The White Birch was used by Aboriginal people in making canoes.

Plant
Wheat is the province's most important crop.

Black bear, moose, elk, caribou and lynx live in the Boreal Forest of spruce, fir and pine.

In the north the Canadian Shield is covered with forests of small spruce and low bushes. Marshes provide nesting grounds for ducks and geese.

Three major river systems cross the province: the Saskatchewan, the Qu'Appelle and the Churchill.

The Qu'Appelle River Valley is an area of fertile farmland running east-west through the dry prairie grasslands.

Churchill R.

North Saskatchewan R.

South Saskatchewan R.

Qu'Appelle R.

PRINCE ALBERT

SASKATOON

REGINA

MOOSEJAW

CYPRESS HILLS

BIG MUDDY BADLANDS

The prairie used to be covered in tall grasses. Now it is used for growing wheat.

In the Big Muddy Badlands, streams have carved the soft rock into strange shapes called hoodoos. Because most of the soil has been washed away, there is little plant life.

The Cypress Hills include the highest point of land between the Rocky Mountains and Labrador.

PEOPLE, PLACES AND EVENTS

W.O. Mitchell was born and raised in Weyburn and is famous for his novel about prairie life, *Who Has Seen the Wind*.

Saskatoon berries were an important fruit for the Aboriginal people and early settlers. Today they are baked into pies as a local treat.

Early pioneers built their homes from sod (strips of grass and earth cut from the ground) because there were so few trees.

The Royal Canadian Mounted Police's world-famous Musical Ride grew out of precision horse-riding drills taught at their training centre in Regina.

HISTORY OF THE PROVINCE

For thousands of years Chipewyan, Beaver and Slavey Nations hunted caribou and trapped beaver in the northern forests. Cree and Blackfoot lived both in the forests and on the central prairies. In the dry southern section, the Assiniboine and the Gros Ventre hunted the bison, also called plains buffalo, for food, and made tipis from their hides.

1700s

From the 1700s into the 1880s, Europeans traded for beaver pelts with the Aboriginal people and built forts. By 1870 the Canadian government was encouraging settlers to take up farmland on the prairies in the southern section. Once the railway was built, settlement speeded up.

1885

Métis (people of French and Aboriginal background) were already settled around Battleford on the Saskatchewan River when hundreds of settlers began arriving from the east. Afraid that they would lose their lands, the Métis, led by Louis Riel, rebelled.

They were defeated by government troops brought in on the new railway.

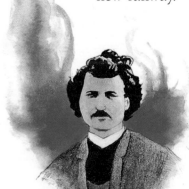

Grey Owl (1888–1938), an Englishman who was made an honorary Ojibwa, was a conservationist who worked to save the beaver population. His cabin is now a museum in Prince Albert National Park.

Gordie Howe, born in Floral, holds the record for most seasons in the National Hockey League (26). He was the greatest hockey player of his time.

Jeanne Sauvé (1922–93), the first woman to be named governor general of Canada, was born in Prud'homme. She was governor general from 1984 to 1990.

More than a thousand grain elevators used to dot the prairie landscape. Farmers brought their wheat to them to be graded and stored until the train arrived. Now most grain is transported by truck.

1905

When Canada needed people who knew how to farm grasslands, the government advertised in Ukraine, Hungary and Russia. Thousands of farm families flocked to the new country. By 1905 prairie settlers wanted a say in local government, so two provinces, Saskatchewan and Alberta, were created.

1930

The prairie farmers prospered until the 1930s. Then, several years with almost no rainfall turned farmland into blowing dust that produced no crops. A worldwide depression meant the government had no money to help the farmers. Many abandoned their farms to look for work elsewhere.

1943

In 1943 Saskatchewan's fortunes improved with the discovery of potash, a chemical used to make fertilizers. By the 1970s oil and uranium ore had also been found.

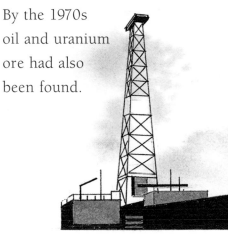

TODAY

Although Saskatchewan no longer has to depend on wheat alone to support itself, it is still known as "the breadbasket of Canada."

MANITOBA

Manitoba's name is thought to come from the Cree words *Manitou bou,* which mean "place of the Great Spirit." This describes the narrows of Lake Manitoba, where waves crashing on rocks sound like the beating of a giant drum. Manitoba is in the middle of Canada and shares the woodland and lake landscape of Ontario to its east and the grasslands of Saskatchewan to its west. To the north it has a sea coast on Hudson Bay. Immigrants to Manitoba came from many countries, including Britain, France, Iceland, Ukraine, Russia, Holland and Germany. In the early years they raised wheat on the grasslands in the south. Later, lumbering and mining in the vast forests to the north became important. Today the manufacturing of such goods as food, paper products, transportation equipment and electrical equipment is the most important industry. Manitoba is known for its long, harsh winters and strong prairie winds.

Motto

GLORIOSUS ET LIBER
(Glorious and Free)

Quick facts

Population: 1 113 898

Size: 649 950 km^2
(250 965 sq. mi.)

Capital city: Winnipeg
(pop. 667 209)

Other major cities:
Brandon (pop. 40 581)
Portage la Prairie
(pop. 20 385)
Thompson (pop. 14 385)

Main industries:
manufacturing, agriculture,
mining

Entered Confederation:
July 15, 1870

Coat of arms

On the shield are the cross of St. Andrew, from the Hudson's Bay Company coat of arms, and a bison. The beaver holds the provincial flower, while the unicorn's collar features a wheel from a Red River cart, and the horse's collar includes the Aboriginal circle of life. At the bottom are wheat, the provincial flower and tree, and water.

Flag

Manitoba's flag is much like the Red Ensign, which used to be the official flag of Canada. The provincial shield has been added on the right side.

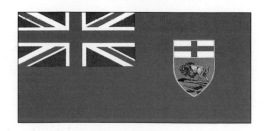

Flower

The flowers of the Prairie Crocus appear so early in the spring that they grow fine hair to protect them from the cold.

Bird

The Great Gray Owl hunts mice and rabbits at night.

Tree

The strong fibres of the White Spruce are important for paper making.

In the harsh, cold climate of the Taiga Shield only dwarf willow and other small trees grow.

A mixture of grasslands and evergreen forests cover the Boreal Plains.

Elk roam through the grasslands and evergreen forests of the Boreal Plains.

Churchill is called the "polar bear capital of the world" because of the large numbers of bears that make their dens south of the town.

Abundant wheat crops grow in the rich, black soil of the flat, grassy prairie.

Thick stands of white and black spruce grow on the Boreal Shield. Forestry, and nickel and copper mining are important industries here.

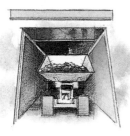

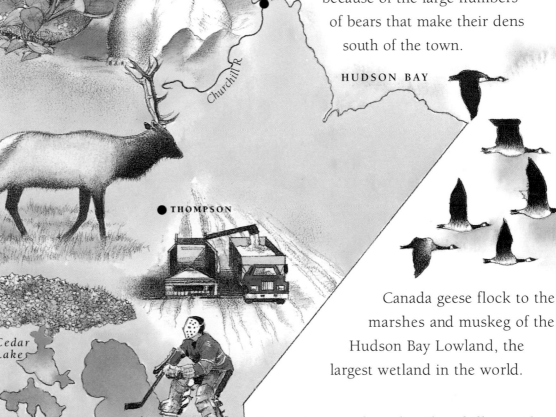

Canada geese flock to the marshes and muskeg of the Hudson Bay Lowland, the largest wetland in the world.

Large rivers such as the Churchill provide energy for hydroelectric projects.

Lake Agassiz, a huge glacial lake, once covered the south-central area of the province.

Thousands of lakes provide homes for the many birds and fish.

PEOPLE, PLACES AND EVENTS

In the early days, Red River carts were used to move freight. Made of wood and hide with no metal parts, the two-wheeled vehicles could be floated across rivers.

Golden Boy, a statue on the dome of the legislative buildings in Winnipeg, holds a torch to signify progress and a sheaf of wheat to show how important agriculture is to the province.

For over 200 years the velvety undercoat of the beaver's fur was used to make felt hats for European gentlemen.

Riding Mountain National Park has a protected herd of bison, once nearly extinct because of overhunting.

HISTORY OF THE PROVINCE

Manitoba's first inhabitants were Plains Nations. Because they followed the bison and caribou, they lived in easily moved tipis. In the far north, Inuit hunted polar bears and seals. Europeans searching for the Northwest Passage to China reached Manitoba through Hudson Bay as early as 1612.

FORT PRINCE OF WALES

1670

In 1670 King Charles II of England granted a huge tract called Rupert's Land to the Hudson's Bay Company, a group of businessmen interested in the fur trade. Along the major rivers flowing into Hudson Bay, they set up trading posts such as York Factory and Fort Prince of Wales at Churchill.

1733

Between 1733 and 1738 the La Verendrye family, explorers from New France (Quebec), travelled the Great Lakes and river systems until they reached the Red and Winnipeg Rivers. Soon after them came traders from the North West Company. Using voyageurs with swift canoes to deliver beaver pelts to Montreal, these traders competed fiercely with the Hudson's Bay Company.

Nellie McClung (1873–1951), a teacher and writer, fought successfully for the rights of women from 1911 to the 1930s. She felt that "the economic dependence of women is the greatest injustice that has been done us." She helped win the case that declared women "persons" and able to sit as judges and in the Senate.

The statue of a giant Viking staring out over Lake Winnipeg reminds visitors of the Viking ancestors of the Icelandic people who settled around Gimli.

Cree artist Jackson Beardy (1944–84), who was born at the Garden Hill Reserve on Island Lake, told the myths and legends of his people through his art.

The green garbage bag was first developed in Winnipeg. In the 1950s Harry Wasylyk needed a cheap way to package fruits and vegetables so he tried a new material called polyethylene.

1811

In 1811 Scottish farmers, led by Lord Selkirk, settled in the Red River Valley. Their fenced farms interfered with the roaming life of the Plains Nations and Métis (people who are part Aboriginal, part French) as they hunted the bison. Although this led to some violence, the Selkirk settlement survived.

1870

In 1870 Canada bought Rupert's Land from the Hudson's Bay Company. As settlers began to flood in, the Métis and their leader, Louis Riel, seized Upper Fort Garry (now Winnipeg) and demanded laws to protect their French language and Roman Catholic schools. As a result, on July 15, 1870, Manitoba (then a tiny area around the Red River Valley) became Canada's fifth province.

1890s

In the 1890s the railway opened more of the country to farmers, miners and lumbermen. By 1912 the Manitoba boundaries had been extended north to Hudson Bay and the 60th parallel. Many factories opened in the cities. In 1919 tension between workers and owners led to the Winnipeg General Strike. After World War II (1939–45), more industrial plants opened.

TODAY

Raising wheat, canola and oats is an important part of Manitoba's economy, but manufacturing and construction are now the province's most important industries.

ONTARIO

Ontario means "beautiful lake" in the Iroquois language, and that's a good name for a province with 250 000 lakes. It is Canada's second-largest province and has the largest population. Ninety per cent of Ontario's people live in the southern part of the province, which is also home to most of Ontario's agriculture and manufacturing industry. Northern Ontario, with 90 per cent of the province's land area, is rich in forests, minerals and hydroelectric power. Mines around Sudbury are the largest source of nickel in the world. This area also produces more copper than any other part of Canada. Ontario stretches from Hudson Bay in the north down to the Great Lakes, which form its southern border with the United States. The climate is mostly sunny with moderate rainfall, swinging from very cold in winter to very warm in summer.

Motto

UT INCEPIT FIDELIS SIC PERMANET
(Loyal it began, loyal it remains)

Quick facts

Population: 10 753 573

Size: 1 068 580 km^2
(412 610 sq. mi.)

Capital city: Toronto
(pop. 4 263 757)

Other major cities:
Ottawa (pop. 763 426)
London (pop. 398 616)
Thunder Bay (pop. 125 562)

Main industries:
manufacturing, agriculture,
mining, forestry

Entered Confederation:
July 1, 1867

Coat of arms

The cross of St. George, England's patron saint, shows Ontario's early links to England. The three maple leaves stand for Canada. The shield is surrounded by a moose, a black bear and a deer.

Flag

Ontario's flag is much like the Red Ensign, which was once Canada's national flag. The British flag in the corner is a reminder of Ontario's early connection to that country. The provincial shield is on the right side.

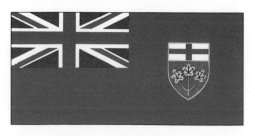

Flower
The White Trillium is found in large numbers in woodlands in early spring.

Bird
The Common Loon is found on lakes in northern Ontario.

Tree
White Pine forests once covered most of southern Ontario.

Gem
The purple amethyst is mined near Thunder Bay.

Two-thirds of Ontario is covered by the Canadian Shield, an area rich in precious metals such as gold, silver and platinum and other metals such as nickel and copper.

The Boreal Forest, an area of spruce, fir and other evergreens, covers half the province, including most of northern Ontario. The trees are used to make more than one-fifth of Canada's newsprint.

HUDSON BAY

JAMES BAY

The Hudson Bay Lowland is covered with muskeg, a spongy carpet of mosses and lichens.

Five national parks and 241 provincial parks, including Algonquin Park, provide areas for fishing, canoeing, skiing and other outdoor sports.

THUNDER BAY

Lake Superior

Four of the five Great Lakes, which together make up the largest body of fresh water in the world, form part of Ontario's border.

OTTAWA

ALGONQUIN PARK

St. Lawrence R.

Lake Huron

Lake Michigan

Lake Ontario

TORONTO

NIAGARA FALLS

The CN Tower in Toronto is 550 m (1800 ft.) high, the world's tallest free-standing structure. At the foot of the tower is SkyDome, the home of World Series champions, the Toronto Blue Jays.

POINT PELEE NATIONAL PARK

LONDON

Lake Erie

Point Pelee on Lake Erie is the warmest and most southerly part of Canada's mainland. It is an important stopover for migrating birds and Monarch butterflies.

Niagara Falls, with the world's largest flow of water per second, has been harnessed to create electricity. Niagara means "thunder of water" in the language of the Neutral Nation.

The Great Lakes–St. Lawrence Lowland contains much of Ontario's best farmland, which grows most of Canada's fruit and vegetables.

PEOPLE, PLACES AND EVENTS

In 1811 John McIntosh of Dundas County found and cultivated a wild apple tree with very sweet fruit. Every McIntosh apple sold today is a direct descendant of that same tree.

On January 22, 1992, Dr. Roberta Bondar became Canada's first female astronaut when the space shuttle *Discovery* began its eight days in orbit around the Earth. Dr. Bondar was born in Sault Ste. Marie.

The game of basketball was invented by John Naismith from Almonte. For the first games he used half-bushel peach baskets with the bottoms cut out.

In a Toronto laboratory Frederick Banting (1891–1941) and Charles Best (1899–1978) developed insulin, a drug that saves the lives of people with diabetes. In 1923 the Nobel Prize was awarded for this discovery.

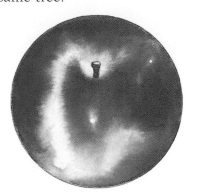

HISTORY OF THE PROVINCE

Since prehistoric times, many Aboriginal peoples lived in the area now called Ontario. By 1600 two groups had settled there. In the north the Ojibwa, Nipissing and Algonquin lived by hunting and gathering. The Huron, Neutral, Petun and Mississauga raised corn and squash in the south.

1630

French explorer Étienne Brûlé arrived in 1630 to live among the Hurons. In 1639 Jesuit missionaries set up a mission at Sainte-Marie among the Hurons on Georgian Bay. French forts often became city sites. Kingston, for example, grew from Fort Frontenac. In 1763, when the British won the Seven Years' War in Europe, they also won France's colonies in North America.

1781

In 1781 Loyalists fleeing the American Revolution settled on the north shore of Lake Ontario. Because of the increase in population, Britain divided Quebec into Upper and Lower Canada. York (now Toronto) was chosen as the capital of Upper Canada (later Ontario). When Americans invaded during the War of 1812, the Canadians were able to repel them.

Emily Stowe (1831–1903) from Norwich was the first woman to practise medicine in Canada. She opened her office in Toronto in 1867.

St. Catharines is the home of the world's first zipper.

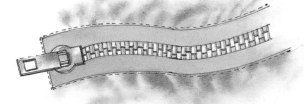

Hockey star Wayne Gretzky first picked up a hockey stick in his hometown of Brantford. Gretzky is one of the only players to be named most valuable player during his first year in the NHL, when he played for Edmonton.

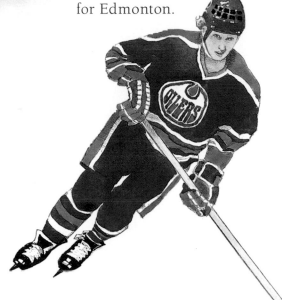

Yonge Street is the longest street in the world. It starts in Toronto at Lake Ontario and runs north and west for 1900 km (1180 mi.) to Rainy River on the Ontario–Minnesota border.

1837

In 1837 the colonists demanded self-government. When Britain refused, journalist William Lyon Mackenzie led a rebellion. The rebels were defeated, but by 1841 the settlers were granted the right to make local laws.

1867

On July 1, 1867, Ontario became one of the first four provinces of the new Dominion of Canada. Uniting meant more protection from invasion and more opportunities to sell produce. Farming and lumbering were Ontario's biggest industries, and in 1883 nickel and copper were discovered in Sudbury.

1914

During World War I (1914–18), the steel and manufactured goods industries grew in Ontario. Although the Great Depression of the 1930s caused much hardship, World War II (1939–45) was good for manufacturing. After the war, the automobile industry and other manufacturing made Ontario an important trade centre.

TODAY

In recent years, immigration has made Ontario a richly multicultural society.

QUEBEC

Canada's largest province takes its name from an Algonquin word meaning "narrow passage." This describes the narrowing of the St. Lawrence River where it passes Quebec City. In the areas north and south of the river are found the best farmlands, the largest cities, and the majority of the population. Manufacturing, particularly the production of clothing, textiles, food and beverages, is also centred here. In the rocky, forested central area, pulp and paper production and mining are important industries. At the northern tip of the province are barren rocks and bogs. From the Arctic north to the temperate south, Quebec's climate changes dramatically. Summers in the St. Lawrence River area are warm and good for growing crops, but the winters are very cold. The province with the second-largest population, Quebec is Canada's only officially French-speaking province.

Motto

JE ME SOUVIENS
(I remember)

Quick facts

Population: 7 138 795

*Size: 1 540 680 km^2
(594 903 sq. mi.)*

*Capital city: Quebec City
(pop. 671 889)*

*Other major cities:
Montreal (pop. 3 326 510)
Laval (pop. 330 393)
Sherbrooke (pop. 147 384)*

*Main industries:
manufacturing, electric power,
mining, pulp and paper*

*Entered Confederation:
July 1, 1867*

Coat of arms
The symbols on the shield represent the three countries that shaped Quebec's history: the fleur-de-lis (lilies) of royal France; the golden lion of Britain; and the maple leaves of Canada.

Flag
Called the *fleurdelisé*, the flag uses the French royal fleur-de-lis as a reminder that Quebec was first settled by France.

Flower
The Madonna Lily was chosen because it resembles the fleur-de-lis.

Bird
The Snowy Owl's thick coat of feathers helps it survive in the Arctic.

Tree
The wood of the American Elm is used for fine furniture.

Mineral
Asbestos, a grey threadlike mineral, does not burn and can be used as protection from heat.

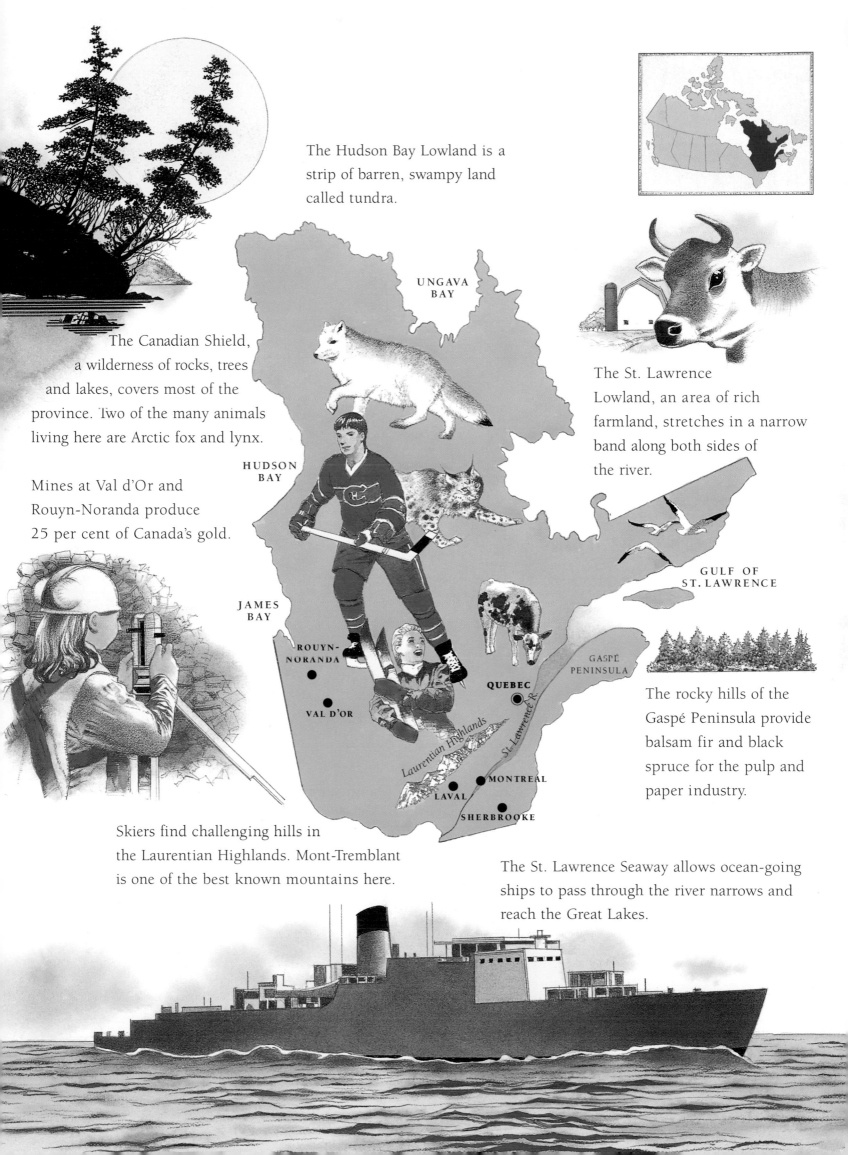

The Hudson Bay Lowland is a strip of barren, swampy land called tundra.

UNGAVA BAY

The Canadian Shield, a wilderness of rocks, trees and lakes, covers most of the province. Two of the many animals living here are Arctic fox and lynx.

HUDSON BAY

Mines at Val d'Or and Rouyn-Noranda produce 25 per cent of Canada's gold.

JAMES BAY

ROUYN-NORANDA

VAL D'OR

The St. Lawrence Lowland, an area of rich farmland, stretches in a narrow band along both sides of the river.

GULF OF ST. LAWRENCE

GASPÉ PENINSULA

QUEBEC

Laurentian Highlands

St-Lawrence R.

MONTREAL

LAVAL

SHERBROOKE

The rocky hills of the Gaspé Peninsula provide balsam fir and black spruce for the pulp and paper industry.

Skiers find challenging hills in the Laurentian Highlands. Mont-Tremblant is one of the best known mountains here.

The St. Lawrence Seaway allows ocean-going ships to pass through the river narrows and reach the Great Lakes.

PEOPLE, PLACES AND EVENTS

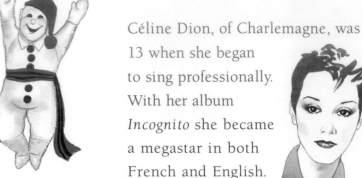

In February, you can meet Bonhomme Carnaval, the king of Quebec's gigantic winter carnival.

Céline Dion, of Charlemagne, was 13 when she began to sing professionally. With her album *Incognito* she became a megastar in both French and English.

Quebec City is the only walled city north of Mexico. Many of the original buildings, dating from 1608, still stand. The United Nations has declared it a World Heritage Site.

Bonaventure Island, a world-famous bird sanctuary, has over 25 000 pairs of gannets.

HISTORY OF THE PROVINCE

1500

The earliest Aboriginal settlers along the St. Lawrence were Iroquois, who grew corn around their villages. They were followed by the Montagnais Nation, (now called Innu) who hunted moose and lived in portable birchbark shelters. Along the shores of Hudson Bay, Inuit have hunted seals and polar bears for centuries.

1534

Jacques Cartier, an explorer, landed at Gaspé in 1534 and claimed the land for France, but it wasn't until Samuel de Champlain arrived in 1608 that a colony, New France, was built. Since the government of France was mostly interested in fur trading, the colony of *habitants* (farmers) grew slowly.

JACQUES CARTIER WAS GREETED BY ABORIGINAL PEOPLE

1601

From 1601 to about 1750, *habitants* farmed in New France and voyageurs travelled the rivers into the continent to trade with Aboriginal people for furs. War broke out between France and Britain, and the walled fortress of Quebec City was captured in 1759 during the Battle of the Plains of Abraham. Britain changed the colony's name to Quebec in 1763.

The Montreal Canadiens have won the Stanley Cup 23 times thanks to stars such as "Rocket" Richard and Jean Béliveau.

J.A. Bombardier (1907–64) of Valcourt, inventor of the snowmobile, produced the first Ski-Doo in 1959.

The game Trivial Pursuit was invented in Montreal and first sold there in 1982.

Reginald Fessenden (1866–1932) of Milton-Est is considered the father of radio. In 1900, he shouted into the microphone of an invention he called "the wireless" and was heard by his assistant 1.5 km (1 mi.) away.

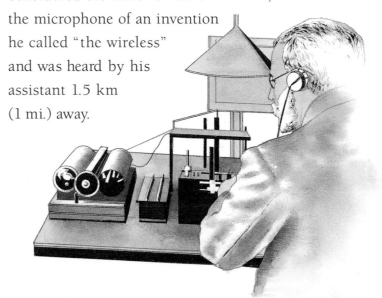

1791

Although Quebec now belonged to Britain, it remained a French-speaking colony until Loyalists fleeing from the American Revolution began arriving, around 1781. Many of these new arrivals settled farther up the river from the French farms and villages, so in 1791 Quebec was divided into Upper Canada (English speaking) and Lower Canada (mainly French speaking).

1837

During the 19th and early 20th centuries, business and government in Quebec were run mainly by British merchants. French resentment against this led to the Patriote Rebellion of 1837. As a result some changes were made, but even becoming one of Canada's founding provinces in 1867 didn't improve life for the French. Most continued to be workers rather than owners of businesses.

1900

After 1900 the growth of manufacturing encouraged people to move to cities. Despite the new jobs, workers soon realized they had few rights. By the 1960s the Quiet Revolution movement was working for change. Workers gained the right to strike, French became the official language and French Canadians called themselves Québécois.

TODAY

Although some Quebeckers want to separate from Canada, a small majority voted in the 1995 Referendum to remain. Their search for a way to be both French and Canadian continues.

NEW BRUNSWICK

New Brunswick is named for George III, who was King of England and Duke of Brunswick when the province was founded in 1784. A small province on the eastern edge of Canada, it has Quebec to the north, the state of Maine on the west, and faces Nova Scotia across the Bay of Fundy. Although the climate in the interior of New Brunswick changes from very cold in winter to very warm in summer, the sea air keeps the coastal areas more moderate.

Industries have grown up around the province's natural resources. There is lumbering in the forested interior, a fisheries industry along the coast, and dairy farming and potato growing in the fertile valley of the Saint John River. New Brunswickers come from a variety of backgrounds, including Scottish and Irish. Many people living on the north shore are French-speaking Acadians. New Brunswick is Canada's only officially bilingual province.

Motto

SPEM REDUXIT

(Hope was restored)

Quick facts

Population: 738 133

Size: 73 440 km^2
(28 360 sq. mi.)

Capital city:
Fredericton (pop. 78 950)

Other major cities:
Saint John (pop. 125 705)
Moncton (pop. 113 491)
Bathurst (pop. 25 415)

Main industries:
manufacturing, mining,
fishing, forestry

Entered Confederation:
July 1, 1867

Coat of arms
An Atlantic Salmon, fiddle-heads, violets and white-tailed deer wearing Indian wampum surround the shield. The royal lion of England prowls across the top of the shield. The bottom has a sailing ship to show how important shipbuilding was in New Brunswick's early days.

Flag
The flag is a rectangular version of the shield.

Flower
The Purple Violet grows in marshy woods and meadows.

Bird
The Black-capped Chickadee feeds on insects, seeds and berries.

Tree
The Balsam Fir is used to make paper.

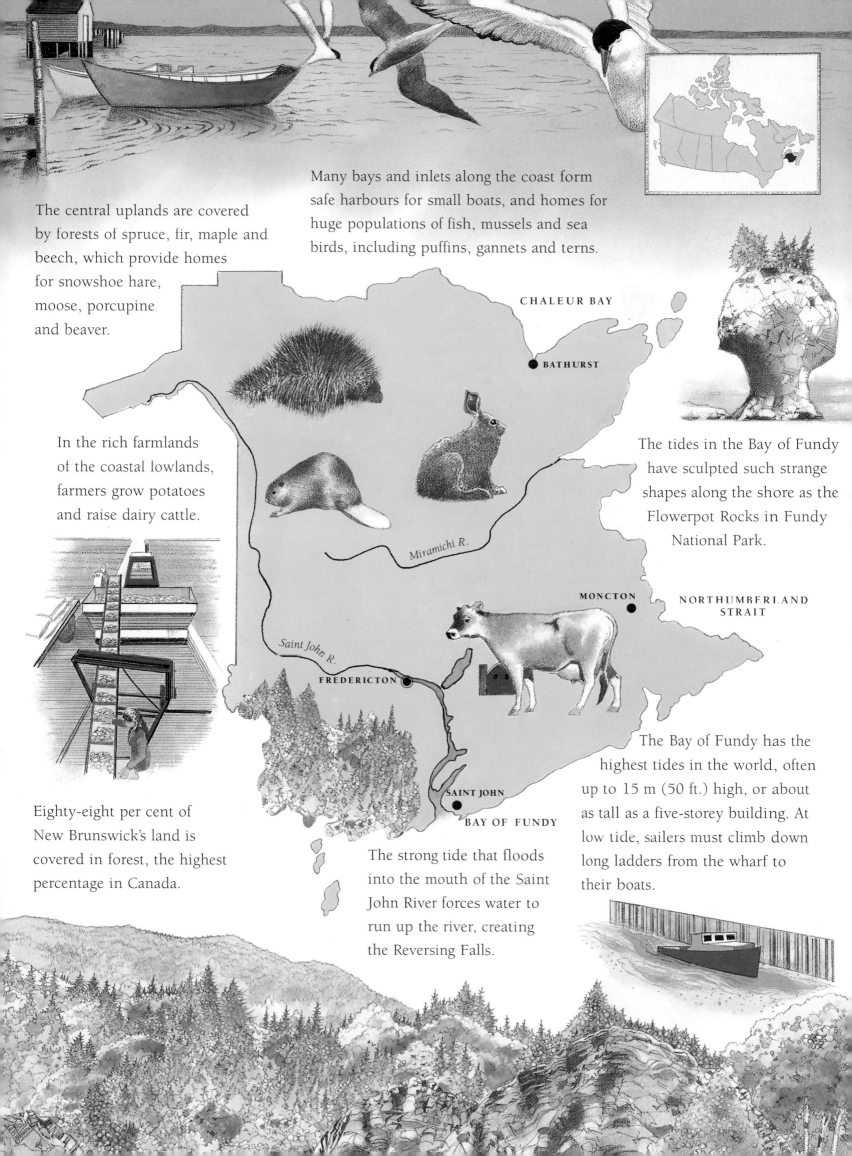

The central uplands are covered by forests of spruce, fir, maple and beech, which provide homes for snowshoe hare, moose, porcupine and beaver.

Many bays and inlets along the coast form safe harbours for small boats, and homes for huge populations of fish, mussels and sea birds, including puffins, gannets and terns.

In the rich farmlands of the coastal lowlands, farmers grow potatoes and raise dairy cattle.

Eighty-eight per cent of New Brunswick's land is covered in forest, the highest percentage in Canada.

CHALEUR BAY

● BATHURST

Miramichi R.

Saint John R.

FREDERICTON ●

MONCTON ●

NORTHUMBERLAND STRAIT

SAINT JOHN ●

BAY OF FUNDY

The strong tide that floods into the mouth of the Saint John River forces water to run up the river, creating the Reversing Falls.

The tides in the Bay of Fundy have sculpted such strange shapes along the shore as the Flowerpot Rocks in Fundy National Park.

The Bay of Fundy has the highest tides in the world, often up to 15 m (50 ft.) high, or about as tall as a five-storey building. At low tide, sailers must climb down long ladders from the wharf to their boats.

PEOPLE, PLACES AND EVENTS

Lobsters are the province's most valuable catch.

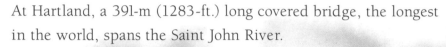

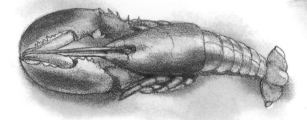

In 1910 the first Canadian chocolate bar was developed at the Ganong chocolate factory in St. Stephen as a quick snack for fishermen.

In 1860 the first steam foghorn sounded from Partridge Island. Invented by engineer Robert Foulis, its hooting was much louder than the clang of a bell. The sound cut through fog and saved many ships.

At Hartland, a 391-m (1283-ft.) long covered bridge, the longest in the world, spans the Saint John River.

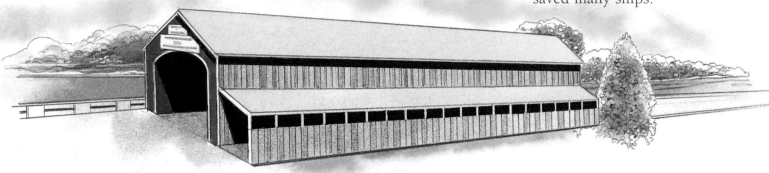

HISTORY OF THE PROVINCE

Early inhabitants of what is now New Brunswick were ancestors of the Micmac and Maliseet Nations who lived by hunting, fishing and gathering plants. These Aboriginal people acted as guides for French explorers, such as Samuel de Champlain in 1604. The French called the east coast area Acadia.

1608

By 1608 French settlers, called Acadians, were farming the land around the Bay of Fundy. Because of warfare in Europe, ownership of Acadia passed back and forth between France and England from 1713 until 1755, when it became permanently English. The Acadians refused to swear loyalty to England, so soldiers burned their homes, and shipped families to far-off places, including Louisiana.

1784

Settlers fleeing from New England during the American Revolution settled along the north shore of the Bay of Fundy and founded the city of Saint John. By 1784 the population in the area was so large that the British government split off the northern section of the original colony of Nova Scotia to create the new colony of New Brunswick.

Roch Voisine of Saint-Basile started composing music at 14. In 1993 he won the Juno Award for male vocalist.

In early spring, New Brunswickers gather the new sprouts of the ostrich fern. Called fiddleheads because of their shape, these ferns are tasty vegetables.

Magnetic Hill is a fascinating optical illusion. When a car is driven to the bottom of the hill, the car seems to coast up the hill. This is because the area is very tilted, so what looks like an upgrade is really a downgrade.

Roméo LeBlanc, born in Memramcook, is the first Acadian to serve as governor general of Canada.

1846

When war with France prevented England from getting lumber from Europe, England turned to New Brunswick for pine to make masts for ships. The timber industry provided work for many, including thousands who arrived after 1846, fleeing famine in Ireland.

1864

By 1864 some politicians were suggesting that the four small British colonies join to form one large country. But England was tired of paying for soldiers to protect the borders against possible American attack, and some colonists wanted larger markets for their crops. On July 1, 1867, New Brunswick became one of the first four provinces of Canada.

1960s

As iron and steel replaced wood for ships, New Brunswick's timber wasn't needed and the province grew poorer and poorer. Throughout the 1960s, an Acadian, Louis Robichaud, was premier. He helped create new jobs by encouraging the growth of such industries as mining and electricity. Robichaud also passed a law making the province officially bilingual.

TODAY

Manufacturing continues to grow as better ways are found to process pulp wood and food products. Telemarketing is a new and growing industry.

NOVA SCOTIA

Nova Scotia means "New Scotland" in Latin. It is a narrow strip of land off the east coast of Canada, attached to New Brunswick by a small land-bridge. At the northern tip is the island of Cape Breton. The indented coastline provides many harbours both for ocean-going ships and for small fishing vessels. Because Nova Scotia is almost surrounded by the sea, fishing has been the province's main industry. Haddock and cod were once caught in great numbers. Today lobster and scallops are the main catches. Timber, coal and oil are also important natural resources. Most of Nova Scotia's population lives near the coast, half of it in the largest cities, Halifax, Dartmouth and Sydney. Although the inland temperatures can range between very cold and very hot, the sea keeps the coastal climate mild. It also causes heavy fogs.

Motto
MUNIT HAEC ET ALTERA VINCIT
(One defends and the other conquers)

Quick facts

Population: 909 282

Size: 55 490 km^2
(21 462 sq. mi.)

Capital city: Halifax
(pop. 332 518)

Other major cities:
Dartmouth (pop. 65 629)
Sydney (pop. 17 294)
Glace Bay (pop. 23 038)

Main industries:
manufacturing, mining,
forestry, fishing

Entered Confederation:
July 1, 1867

Coat of arms
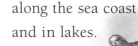
The shield carries the cross of St. Andrew, patron saint of Scotland, and the royal lion of Scotland to show the province's early links to that country. The unicorn also represents Scotland and the Aboriginal hunter represents the Native population.

Flag
The flag is a rectangular version of the shield.

Flower
The Mayflower, or Trailing Arbutus, blooms in woodlands in early spring.

Bird
From high in the sky, Osprey plummet feet first to catch fish along the sea coast and in lakes.

Tree
The Red Spruce is an evergreen used for pulp, paper and lumber.

Gem
Agate is a semiprecious stone sometimes used to make jewellery.

Mineral
Stilbite, a pearly white mineral, is found near the Bay of Fundy.

Cumberland County grows such a huge crop of blueberries each year that it is now the world's largest producer of frozen wild blueberries. Some are made into pies and jam for the annual blueberry festival.

The Continental Shelf is a ledge of rock 200 m (655 ft.) below the surface. It was once the richest fishing ground in the world and teemed with Atlantic Cod and other fish.

The rich farmland of the Annapolis Valley is good for apple growing and dairy farming.

Much of the interior is rocky upland covered with a mixed forest of spruce, maple and birch.

The Bay of Fundy is famous both for its high tides and its scallops, a type of shellfish abundant here.

CABOT TRAIL

CAPE BRETON ISLAND

GLACE BAY

SYDNEY

Bras D'or Lake

LOUISBOURG

NORTHUMBERLAND STRAIT

BAY OF FUNDY

ANNAPOLIS VALLEY

DARTMOUTH

HALIFAX

PEGGY'S COVE

ATLANTIC OCEAN

The lighthouse at Peggy's Cove is one of the hundreds that used to line the coast to warn ships of rocks ahead.

Bras D'Or, a large saltwater lake, is home to 250 pairs of nesting bald eagles. The bald eagle is an endangered species. This lake and the Cabot Trail, an area of spectacular highland scenery, attract tourists to Cape Breton Island.

Alexander Graham Bell, inventor of the telephone, spent summers at Bras D'or Lake on Cape Breton Island, where he tested an early airplane, the *Silver Dart*.

The Atlantic Ocean has cut the coastline into thousands of bays and coves. Fishing vessels with nets for catching cod and herring set out from villages such as Peggy's Cove. Whales are often seen off Nova Scotia's western coast.

PEOPLE, PLACES AND EVENTS

The schooner *Bluenose*, built in Lunenburg, was the fastest ship of her type. Now she is pictured on the Canadian dime.

At Grand Pré, in the Annapolis Valley, a statue of Evangeline, the fictional heroine of a famous poem, reminds visitors of the Acadians who were driven from their homes and farms in 1755.

At Louisbourg, a French fort built to guard the entrance to the St. Lawrence River, visitors experience life in 1744 as they walk through reconstructed buildings and streets.

HISTORY OF THE PROVINCE

From prehistoric times, Aboriginal people have lived in the area now called Nova Scotia. When Europeans arrived in 1605, the Micmac, who lived by fishing, hunting and gathering plants and berries, were there. French settlers called all the land along the Atlantic coast Acadia. Their first settlement was at Port Royal (now Annapolis Royal).

PORT ROYAL

1755

France and England had been fighting in Europe for many years. By 1755 France had not only lost the war but also her colonies in the New World. When Britain ordered the Acadian colonists to swear loyalty to the British Crown most refused. Britain wanted land for its own colonists, so the Acadians were forced off their farms. Some were sent back to France, others to the United States.

1784

Settlers came from many countries. The English founded the city of Halifax and, later, Germans settled in Lunenburg and Scottish Highlanders chose Cape Breton Island. During the American Revolution many Loyalists (people who wanted to live in a British country) came from New England and New York State. By 1784 the colony had grown too large to govern easily, so it was divided into Nova Scotia and New Brunswick.

Singer Ann Murray, from Springhill, earned the first of many gold singles with her recording of "Snowbird."

In 1902 Guglielmo Marconi sent the first west-to-east wireless (radio) message across the Atlantic Ocean from Table Head on Cape Breton Island.

In 1856 Abraham Gesner helped to brighten the world by distilling kerosene from petroleum. This allowed people to replace their dim, smoky candles with brighter and less expensive oil lamps.

The Citadel, a star-shaped fort, sits high on a hill overlooking Halifax harbour. Soldiers in 19th-century uniforms drill on the parade ground.

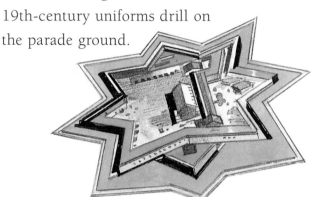

Micmac legends tell many stories of the mighty chief Glooscap, who is said to have shaped the coastline of Nova Scotia as well as creating the Aboriginal people and animals.

1867

As industries such as lumbering and shipbuilding grew, business owners wanted more markets and faster ways to transport goods. They suggested a railway, but this was too expensive for one colony. At the same time the British government wanted to withdraw its soldiers. To pay for an army and a railway, Nova Scotia decided to join with New Brunswick, Canada East and Canada West. On July 1, 1867, the four offically became the Dominion of Canada.

1917

Halifax's large natural harbour makes the city an important seaport. During World War I (1914–18) many Canadian and British ships were based in Halifax Harbour. On December 17, 1917, a ship carrying explosives blew up, killing 1600 and destroying the whole north end of the city.

1950s

The coal mining that made parts of Nova Scotia wealthy in the early 20th century was in decline by the 1950s. By the 1990s, when shrinking cod stocks closed the fish processing plants, Nova Scotia had lost two major industries.

TODAY

Although Nova Scotia has lost such major industries as fishing and fish processing, tourism is growing. Many tourists are drawn to the province each summer by its beauty and history.

PRINCE EDWARD ISLAND

Prince Edward Island was named in 1799 to honour England's Duke of Kent, Queen Victoria's father. Its original name, *Abegweit*, came from a Micmac word meaning "cradled in the waves." The smallest of Canada's provinces in both size and population, this crescent-shaped island lies in the Gulf of St. Lawrence, separated from New Brunswick and Nova Scotia by the Northumberland Strait.

The surrounding sea keeps the temperatures moderate both winter and summer but the constant winds bring many winter storms. Known as "the million-acre farm," the Island is famous worldwide for the 70 varieties of potatoes grown in its rust-coloured soil. Anne of Green Gables, a character created by L.M. Montgomery, has made the Island well known as far away as Japan.

Motto
PARVA SUB INGENTI
(The small under the protection of the great)

Quick facts

Population: 134 557

Size: 5 660 km^2
(2 185 sq. mi.)

Capital city:
Charlottetown (pop. 57 224)

Other centres:
Summerside (pop. 16 001)

Main industries: agriculture, tourism, manufacturing

Entered Confederation:
July 1, 1873

Coat of arms
The royal lion of England stretches across the top. Beneath it a large oak tree and three smaller oaks grow on a green island. The large oak represents England guarding the Island's three counties.

Flag
The flag is a rectangular version of the shield.

Flower

The Lady's-slipper, a type of orchid, blooms in moist, shady woodlands in May and June.

Bird
The loud shriek of the Blue Jay warns other birds of danger.

Tree
The Red Oak is known for its strength and long life.

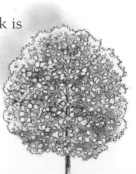

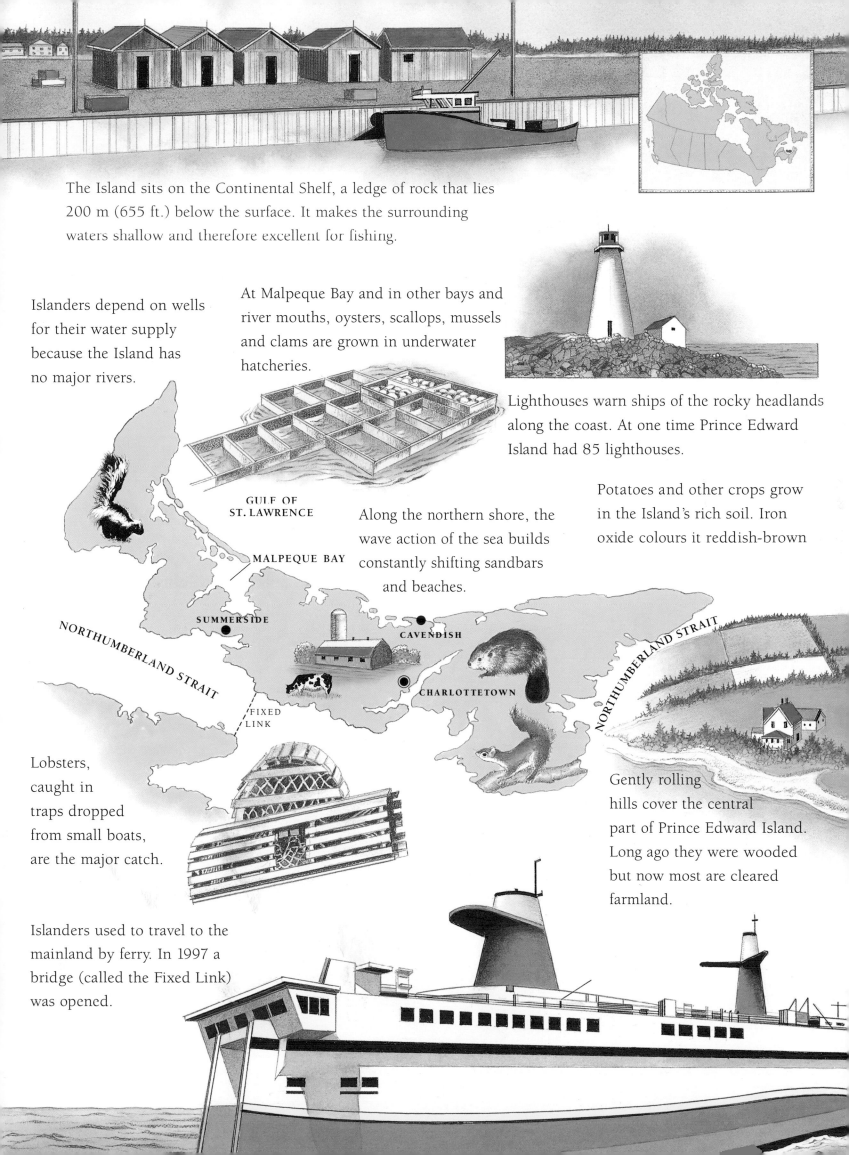

The Island sits on the Continental Shelf, a ledge of rock that lies 200 m (655 ft.) below the surface. It makes the surrounding waters shallow and therefore excellent for fishing.

Islanders depend on wells for their water supply because the Island has no major rivers.

At Malpeque Bay and in other bays and river mouths, oysters, scallops, mussels and clams are grown in underwater hatcheries.

Lighthouses warn ships of the rocky headlands along the coast. At one time Prince Edward Island had 85 lighthouses.

Potatoes and other crops grow in the Island's rich soil. Iron oxide colours it reddish-brown

GULF OF ST. LAWRENCE

Along the northern shore, the wave action of the sea builds constantly shifting sandbars and beaches.

MALPEQUE BAY

NORTHUMBERLAND STRAIT

SUMMERSIDE

CAVENDISH

CHARLOTTETOWN

NORTHUMBERLAND STRAIT

FIXED LINK

Gently rolling hills cover the central part of Prince Edward Island. Long ago they were wooded but now most are cleared farmland.

Lobsters, caught in traps dropped from small boats, are the major catch.

Islanders used to travel to the mainland by ferry. In 1997 a bridge (called the Fixed Link) was opened.

PEOPLE, PLACES AND EVENTS

Every year thousands of tourists visit Cavendish, the setting for Lucy Maud Montgomery's story about the red-haired orphan, Anne of Green Gables.

The world's largest giant bluefin tuna (680 kg [1500 lbs.]) was caught near North Lake Harbour in 1979. Tuna fishing is a popular sport.

Charlottetown is called the "birthplace of Canada." A conference held in Province House in 1864 led, three years later, to the formation of the new country.

HISTORY OF THE PROVINCE

Aboriginal people have lived on the Island for thousands of years. The most recent were the Micmac, who moved from place to place living in moveable huts of skin or bark. In winter they hunted deer in the forest. In summer they moved to the coast to fish for salmon and gather mussels and clams from the shore.

1720

In 1720 the Island was settled by the French, who called it Île St-Jean. When the English took over the Island, the French farmers were forced to leave. Although many were transported first to England and then to Louisiana, some hid in the woods and later turned to fishing to support themselves because they had no land.

1770s

In the 1770s many settlers arrived from Scotland. Loyalists fleeing from the American Revolution came in the 1780s. Besides fishing and farming, shipbuilding became an important industry on the island. In 1769 the colony, called the Island of St. John, was divided from Nova Scotia and in 1799 it was named Prince Edward Island.

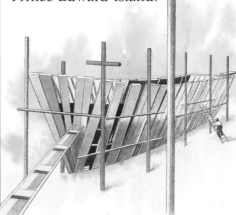

Huge icebreakers keep ferry lanes open in winter.

Irish moss, a type of seaweed, is gathered from the sea floor by horse-drawn sleds after storms. It is used as a thickener in ice cream, toothpaste and other products.

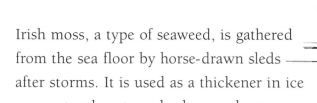

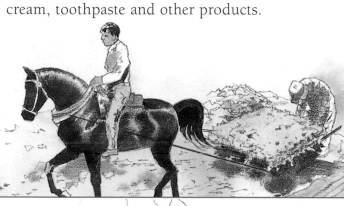

The Confederation Centre, built in 1967 as a Centennial project, has a theatre, library and art gallery.

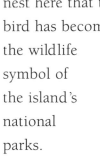

Great blue herons spend spring and summer on the marshes and mudflats. So many nest here that the bird has become the wildlife symbol of the island's national parks.

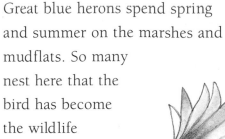

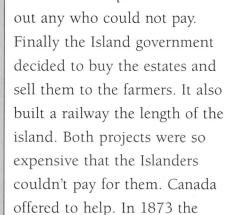

1873

From 1767 on, most of the Island was owned by wealthy men who lived in England. They charged the farmers high rent and were quick to turn out any who could not pay. Finally the Island government decided to buy the estates and sell them to the farmers. It also built a railway the length of the island. Both projects were so expensive that the Islanders couldn't pay for them. Canada offered to help. In 1873 the Island joined Confederation as Canada's seventh province.

1900

By the turn of the century, lobster fishing and the breeding of silver foxes for their pelts had become important industries. As well, the first boxcar-load of seed potatoes had been sold and shipped from Prince Edward Island to start potato crops in other countries. Despite these successes, the Island's agricultural industry provided few new jobs, and from 1891 to the 1930s many people left to find work in Canada's west.

1960

By the 1960s, with help from the federal government, life on the Island was improving. Dairy farming, potato growing and fishing are still important industries.

TODAY

Beautiful scenery and a historic past have made tourism a profitable industry for present-day Prince Edward Island.

NEWFOUNDLAND AND LABRADOR

Canada's most easterly province is made up of two parts, the mainland coastal area of Labrador and the island of Newfoundland. Although the cold Atlantic Ocean constantly crashes against the coast, the warm Gulf Stream swirls past the island, warming the air and making the climate damp and foggy. Waters teeming with fish fed Aboriginal people for thousands of years before European sailors, blown off course, discovered the island and returned to harvest the cod and herring. For 500 years, catching and processing fish have been the main industries both on the island and in the coastal communities of the mainland. Today, overfishing has almost destroyed them. Mining, particularly the production of iron ore, is now the most important industry.

Motto
QUAERITE PRIME REGNUM DEI
(Seek ye first the kingdom of God)

Quick facts

Population: 551 792

Size: 405 720 km^2
(156 660 sq. mi.)

Capital city: St. John's
(pop. 174 051)

Other centres:
Corner Brook (pop. 27 945)
Conception Bay (pop. 19 265)
Gander (pop. 12 021)

Main industries: mining, forestry, manufacturing, hydroelectricity

Entered Confederation:
March 31, 1949

Coat of arms
A silver cross like that of the Knights of St. John divides the shield in four. The unicorns and lions represent England and Scotland. The shield is surrounded by Aboriginal warriors and an elk.

Flag
The golden arrow of hope is combined with a trident showing the province's dependence on the sea. White symbolizes snow and ice; blue, the surrounding sea.

Flower
The insect-eating Pitcher Plant grows in bogs.

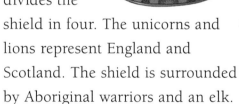

Bird
The Atlantic Puffin, an unofficial symbol, nests on islands along the seashore.

Tree
The Black Spruce is used in many industries, including pulp and paper, and in making musical instruments, such as guitars and violins.

Gem
Labradorite, a type of feldspar, can be identified by its dark blue sheen.

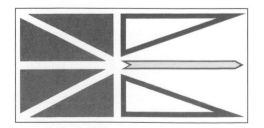

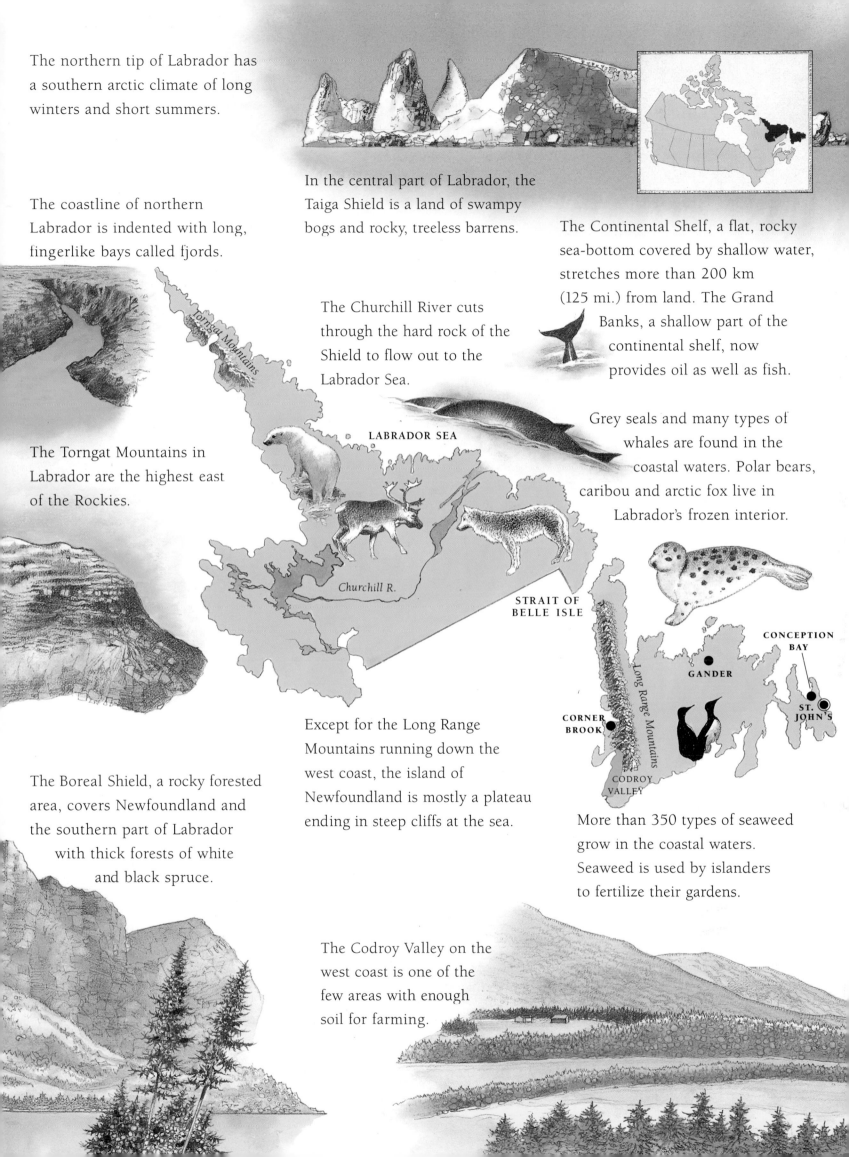

The northern tip of Labrador has a southern arctic climate of long winters and short summers.

The coastline of northern Labrador is indented with long, fingerlike bays called fjords.

In the central part of Labrador, the Taiga Shield is a land of swampy bogs and rocky, treeless barrens.

The Continental Shelf, a flat, rocky sea-bottom covered by shallow water, stretches more than 200 km (125 mi.) from land. The Grand Banks, a shallow part of the continental shelf, now provides oil as well as fish.

The Churchill River cuts through the hard rock of the Shield to flow out to the Labrador Sea.

The Torngat Mountains in Labrador are the highest east of the Rockies.

Grey seals and many types of whales are found in the coastal waters. Polar bears, caribou and arctic fox live in Labrador's frozen interior.

The Boreal Shield, a rocky forested area, covers Newfoundland and the southern part of Labrador with thick forests of white and black spruce.

Except for the Long Range Mountains running down the west coast, the island of Newfoundland is mostly a plateau ending in steep cliffs at the sea.

More than 350 types of seaweed grow in the coastal waters. Seaweed is used by islanders to fertilize their gardens.

The Codroy Valley on the west coast is one of the few areas with enough soil for farming.

LABRADOR SEA

Churchill R.

STRAIT OF BELLE ISLE

CONCEPTION BAY

GANDER

CORNER BROOK

Long Range Mountains

ST. JOHN'S

CODROY VALLEY

Torngat Mountains

PEOPLE, PLACES AND EVENTS

The hydroelectric station at Churchill Falls in Labrador is one of the world's largest producers of electricity.

Hibernia, a large oil-drilling project in the waters of the Grand Banks, is in the path of more than 400 drifting icebergs each year. Small boats stand ready to push them away.

Signal Hill is a high cliff overlooking the Atlantic Ocean. Here, in 1901 Guglielmo Marconi, an Italian inventor, received the first radio message ever to be beamed across the Atlantic Ocean. Cabot Tower sits on Signal Hill overlooking the Atlantic Ocean.

In 1912 the *Titanic*, the largest passenger ship of its day, struck an iceberg just south of Newfoundland. It sank and 1513 people drowned.

Kevin Major, author of seven books for young people, lives in St. John's. His novel *Blood Red Ochre* is a time-travel fantasy about Shawnadithit, the girl who was the last of the Beothuk.

HISTORY OF THE PROVINCE

For thousands of years the ancestors of Inuit hunted seal and polar bears along the coast of Labrador. Aboriginal people called Beothuk hunted caribou and fished in the teeming rivers of the island. The Beothuk are now extinct.

986

Around 986 a Viking sea captain, Bjarni Herjolfsson, was blown off course on his way to Greenland. His tales of a land rich in timber and wild fruit brought other Vikings led by Leif Ericsson. They built the first European settlement at L'Anse aux Meadows, nearly 500 years before Christopher Columbus saw North America in 1492.

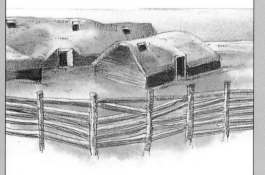

1497

When explorer John Cabot claimed St. John's Isle for King Henry VII of England in 1497, the rich fishing grounds of the Grand Banks were already well known to sailors from France, Spain and Portugal. By 1502 the island was being called New Found Land. For the next two centuries fleets from France, England and other European countries fished the Grand Banks every summer.

In the early 1900s, Wilfred Grenfell, medical doctor and missionary, used a hospital ship to bring medical care to remote fishing villages along the coasts of Labrador and Newfoundland. To help fund this work, he organized rug-making by local artisans. These handmade rugs featured designs of dogsleds, geese and polar bears.

Customs brought from England and Ireland are still popular in Newfoundland. At Christmastime, groups of mummers, masqueraders in fancy dress, travel around the villages singing songs and performing amusing plays. Often they are invited in for a party.

In 1866, Heart's Content was the North American landing point for the first transatlantic telegraph cable. Laid along the seabed, this cable made it possible to send messages quickly from Britain to North America.

Cape St. Mary's is a bird sanctuary where thousands of seabirds nest on rocks and cliffs overlooking the ocean.

Cape Spear is the place in North America that is closest to Europe.

1634

Beginning in 1634, the colony was ruled by fishing admirals. The captain of the first English fishing boat to arrive each spring became Admiral for the season, and he was responsible for keeping law and order. It wasn't until 1832 that an elected local government was established in St. John's, the largest settlement. The distinctive accent of Newfoundlanders comes from the English and Irish settlers who built small villages along the coast.

1867

Newfoundland decided not to join the new country of Canada in 1867. It felt there was no need: The fisheries provided many jobs in the small outport villages; mining, logging and farming were growing; and a new railway made travel easier. The people felt secure as an independent country, first in the British Empire and later in the Commonwealth.

1930s

The Great Depression of the 1930s created much hardship and the country had to become a British colony once more. Although World War II (1939–45) brought jobs to the island and an airport to Goose Bay in Labrador, a group led by Joey Smallwood wanted to join Canada. In 1949 Newfoundland became Canada's tenth province.

TODAY

In the 1960s and 1970s new industries developed in the province but the shrinking supply of cod brought more unemployment in the 1990s. The Hibernia oil fields promise hope for the future.

YUKON TERRITORY

Yukon Territory was named for the majestic river that flows through it. In the language of the Kutchin, the Aboriginal people of that area, *Yu-kun-ah* means "great river." Yukon Territory occupies Canada's most northwesterly corner. This area of mountains and rivers provides tourists with exciting wilderness trips to such spectacular sights as the Kluane Ice Fields and the Chilkoot Trail. Although the climate ranges from mild in summer to subzero in winter, the bright sun and dry air make skiing, dogsledding and snowshoeing enjoyable sports. Ever since the gold rush of 1898, mining has been the major industry. Today about two-thirds of the residents live in the capital city, Whitehorse.

Motto
None

Quick facts

Population: 30 766

*Size: 483 450 km²
(186 675 sq. mi.)*

*Capital city: Whitehorse
(pop. 23 474)*

*Other centres:
Dawson (pop.1999)
Watson Lake (pop. 1794)*

*Main industries:
mining, tourism*

*Entered Confederation:
June 13, 1898*

Coat of arms
Wavy white lines on a blue background stand for the rivers of the Yukon, red triangles for its mountains and yellow circles for its mineral wealth. The malamute dog represents courage, loyalty and stamina. In the centre of the cross of St. George, patron saint of England, is a medallion recalling the interest early explorers had in the fur trade.

Flag
The three colours represent the Territory's major features: green for the taiga forests, white for snow and blue for water. On the white panel, stems of fireweed are crossed under the shield.

Flower
Fireweed is usually the first plant to appear after a forest fire.

Bird
The Common Raven is an important spiritual symbol for the Aboriginal people.

Gem
Lazulite is a deep blue stone used in jewellery making.

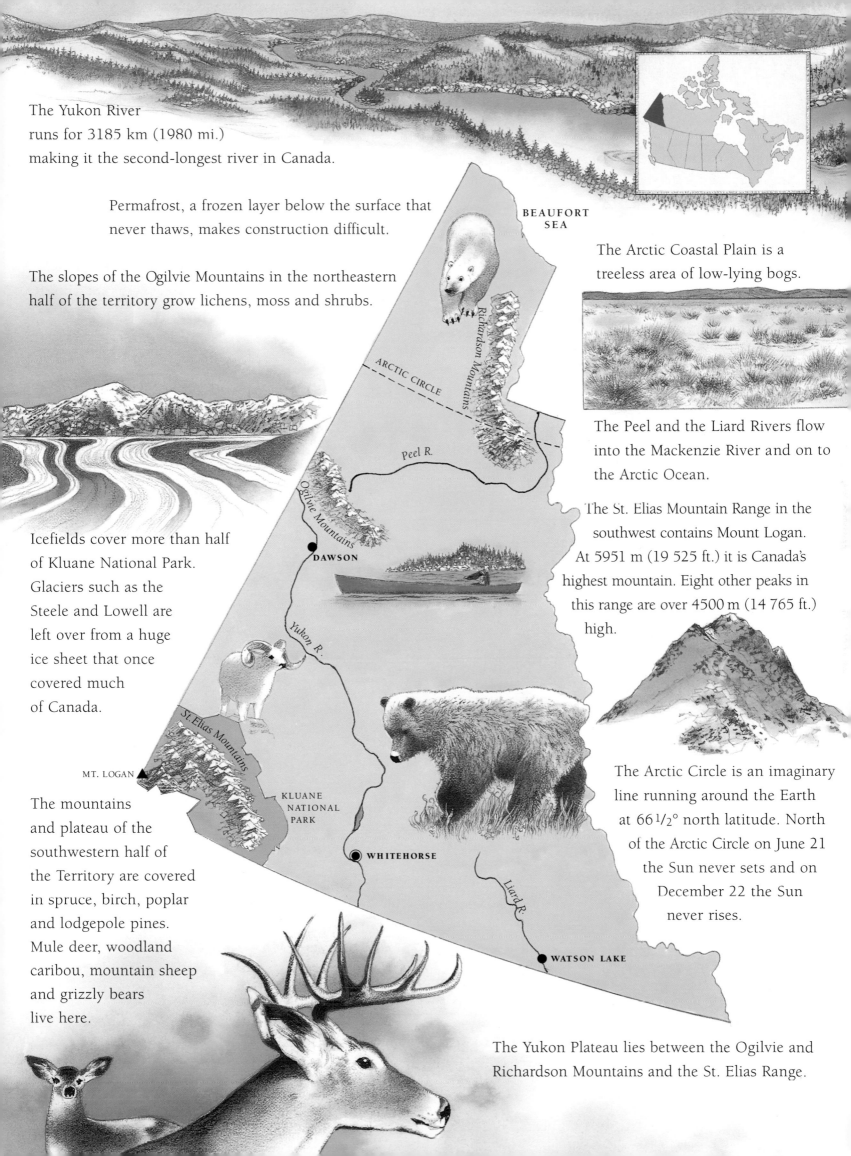

The Yukon River runs for 3185 km (1980 mi.) making it the second-longest river in Canada.

Permafrost, a frozen layer below the surface that never thaws, makes construction difficult.

The slopes of the Ogilvie Mountains in the northeastern half of the territory grow lichens, moss and shrubs.

Icefields cover more than half of Kluane National Park. Glaciers such as the Steele and Lowell are left over from a huge ice sheet that once covered much of Canada.

The mountains and plateau of the southwestern half of the Territory are covered in spruce, birch, poplar and lodgepole pines. Mule deer, woodland caribou, mountain sheep and grizzly bears live here.

BEAUFORT SEA

ARCTIC CIRCLE

Richardson Mountains

Peel R.

Ogilvie Mountains

DAWSON

Yukon R.

St. Elias Mountains

MT. LOGAN

KLUANE NATIONAL PARK

WHITEHORSE

Liard R.

WATSON LAKE

The Arctic Coastal Plain is a treeless area of low-lying bogs.

The Peel and the Liard Rivers flow into the Mackenzie River and on to the Arctic Ocean.

The St. Elias Mountain Range in the southwest contains Mount Logan. At 5951 m (19 525 ft.) it is Canada's highest mountain. Eight other peaks in this range are over 4500 m (14 765 ft.) high.

The Arctic Circle is an imaginary line running around the Earth at $66 1/2°$ north latitude. North of the Arctic Circle on June 21 the Sun never sets and on December 22 the Sun never rises.

The Yukon Plateau lies between the Ogilvie and Richardson Mountains and the St. Elias Range.

PEOPLE, PLACES AND EVENTS

During the Gold Rush, Martha Louise Black (1866–1957) walked and canoed through the rugged country and even hiked alone across the steep Chilkoot Pass into the Klondike. In 1936 she became Canada's second female member of Parliament.

"Sourdough" (a type of bread used on the frontier) was the name given to a prospector who had made it through at least one winter in the gold fields. Inexperienced newcomers were called "Cheechakos."

Beaver Creek, near the Yukon's border with Alaska, is Canada's most westerly community.

In 1995 the Royal Canadian Mounted Police celebrated 100 years in the Yukon. Just 22 men arrived the first year to keep law and order among thousands of gold seekers.

At Watson Lake there is a forest of signposts. In 1942 a homesick road-builder working on the Alaska Highway put up a sign pointing towards his home. Today over 20 000 signs point to such faraway places as Tokyo and Quebec City.

HISTORY OF THE TERRITORY

Over 12 000 years ago people crossed the Bering Strait from Asia and migrated here. Inuit hunted and fished along the Arctic coast. South of them, Kutchin, Tutchone, Tagish and Inland Tlingit Nations lived by trapping and hunting. The smallpox germ, carried by trade goods from the Alaskan coast, wiped out many of these people before the first Europeans arrived.

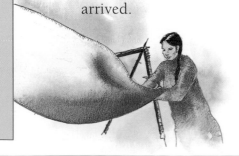

1741

Russia claimed Alaska in 1741. During the next 30 years Russian explorers traded with the Inuit east of Alaska. Fearing Russia would try to claim the whole of the North, Britain signed a treaty in 1825 agreeing on the present boundary between Alaska and the Yukon. From 1825 to 1847 the English explorer Sir John Franklin searched for the Northwest Passage, a route to China.

1842

The Hudson's Bay Company built Fort Frances in 1842 and Fort Selkirk in 1848 to trade for furs with the Aboriginal people. By the 1860s missionaries were establishing churches and scientists were studying the wildlife and mineral wealth of the north.

In the early days thousands of prospectors travelled from Whitehorse to Dawson by riverboat. The last of the stern-wheelers, the SS *Klondike*, is now a museum.

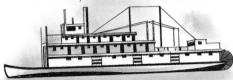

In 1989 Audrey McLaughlin, member of Parliament for the Yukon, became the leader of the national New Democratic Party (NDP) and the first woman to lead a national party.

Robert W. Service (1874–1958) was nicknamed "the poet of the Yukon" after he published poems about life during the Klondike Gold Rush. Most famous are *The Shooting of Dan McGrew* and *The Cremation of Sam McGee.*

English painter Ted Harrison found the Yukon landscape so inspiring that he experimented with unusual colours and shapes to create a new style. His work can be seen in his illustrated version of *The Cremation of Sam McGee.*

1896

Gold was discovered at Forty Mile Creek in 1896, but the rush didn't start until 1898. That year, near the Klondike River, prospectors found gold in large flakes that they could pick easily from the rocks. Soon thousands more gold seekers arrived. In 1898 Yukon became a federal territory with Dawson as the capital city.

1899

Almost overnight more than a thousand prospectors pitched tents in Dawson near the gold fields. With them came saloon-keepers, merchants and the North-West Mounted Police. By 1899 the gold that could be mined easily was almost gone. Dawson shrank as quickly as it had grown.

1900

By 1900, only companies with expensive equipment could mine for gold, copper, lead and zinc. Whaling in the Beaufort Sea lasted until 1914, when whale oil was no longer needed for lighting. The population shrank steadily. Then, in 1942 the United States decided to build the Alaska Highway through the Yukon. Hundreds of labourers arrived in Whitehorse, which soon replaced Dawson as the capital.

TODAY

The fur trade still plays an important part in the Yukon's economy but mining and tourism now provide most of the jobs in the territory.

NORTHWEST TERRITORIES

The Northwest Territories cover a vast area north of the 60th parallel of latitude. Including the Arctic Islands and the mainland, they make up more than 34 per cent of Canada's total area but only 1 per cent of its population. The Territories are larger than Quebec, Canada's largest province. In this immense land of ice, snow, mountains and plains live small populations of Inuit, Dene (pronounced *Den-ay*) and Métis. Most people who came here from the south live in Yellowknife. Many work in the mining and petroleum industries. The climate ranges from extremely cold and dry in the far north to mild summers and cold winters in the southern sections. The Northwest Territories will soon become two independent regions. On April 1, 1999, the northeastern section, Nunavut (Our Land), will become a self-governing Inuit community. The self-government date for the southwestern section, Denedeh (Land of the People), has not yet been chosen.

Motto
None

Quick facts

Population: 64 402

Size: 3 426 320 km²
(1 323 000 sq. mi.)

Capital City:
Yellowknife (pop. 17 275)

Other centres:
Inuvik (pop. 3296)
Hay River (pop. 3611)
Iqaluit (pop. 4220)

Main industries:
construction, mining, tourism

Entered Confederation:
July 15, 1870

Coat of arms
The wavy blue line shows the Northwest Passage cutting through the Arctic ice. The green section, representing trees, and the red, for tundra, include gold rectangles and a fox to show minerals and furs. The narwhals flank a "compass rose" representing the North Pole.

Flag
The white panel stands for snow and ice. The two blue panels show the abundant water of the Territories.

Flower
The Mountain Avens, a type of rose, grows on rocky ground in the Arctic.

Tree
The Jack Pine grows farthest north of all the pines.

Mineral
Gold is mined near Yellowknife.

All the islands north of the uneven dotted line are part of the Arctic Archipelago. In the short summer, lichen and other small plants appear on the islands.

Inukshuit, stone towers built to look like humans, were used to herd caribou towards waiting hunters.

The treeline, the line above which it is too cold for trees to grow, divides the Territories into arctic and subarctic regions.

The Mackenzie River, running from Great Slave Lake north 4241 km (2635 mi.) to the Beaufort Sea, is Canada's longest river.

ARCTIC OCEAN

ELLESMERE ISLAND

BEAUFORT SEA

INUVIK

Mackenzie R.

Mackenzie Mountains

Franklin Mountains

Great Bear Lake

Great Slave Lake

YELLOWKNIFE

HAY RIVER

WOOD BUFFALO NATIONAL PARK

THE BARREN LANDS

ARCTIC CIRCLE

BAFFIN ISLAND

IQALUIT

HUDSON BAY

Baffin Island, Canada's largest island, is the winter home of beluga whales and a nesting ground for gulls and murres.

The blue line indicates the border of Nunavut.

The Mackenzie and Franklin Mountain Ranges run along the border with the Yukon.

The Mackenzie River Valley is an area of muskeg and swamps. Black spruce grow on the hillsides.

The Lowland Plains are dotted with many lakes. The swampy grasslands here are mixed with forests of spruce and tamarack.

The southern Arctic is part of the Canadian Shield. Areas that were scraped down to bare rock by ancient glaciers are known as the Barren Lands.

At 614 m (2015 ft.) deep, Great Slave Lake is Canada's deepest lake. Great Bear Lake is the largest lake completely inside Canada.

PEOPLE, PLACES AND EVENTS

The Dempster Highway, running for 700 km (435 mi.) from Dawson to Inuvik, is the only public highway north of the Arctic Circle. A special gravel bed protects the road from the heaving of the permafrost below.

Pingos, cone-shaped mounds of solid ice covered with soil and plants, are pushed out of the tundra by permafrost action. Hundreds are found on the Mackenzie River Delta. Some are 70 m (230 ft.) high.

Soapstone, which has a slippery texture that feels like soap, has been used by Inuit for centuries to carve such useful utensils as lamps. Today the sale of soapstone sculpture is an important industry.

Ellesmere National Park Reserve on Ellesmere Island is the world's most northerly park.

HISTORY OF THE TERRITORIES

Over 12 000 years ago ancestors of the Dene Nation crossed the Bering Strait from Siberia and moved south where they hunted caribou. Later, ancestors of the Inuit followed, living first in Alaska, then moving to the Canadian Arctic. They became expert at hunting seal and polar bears.

LEIF ERICSSON

1000

Around A.D. 1000 the Norse adventurer Leif Ericsson, sailing from Greenland, may have been the first European to visit this area. In 1576 Sir Martin Frobisher arrived hoping to find a northern route to China. When he failed, Europe lost interest in the area for 200 years.

1771

With the fur traders came explorers. In 1771 Samuel Hearne travelled as far as Great Slave Lake, where he named Yellowknife after the copper knives used by the Aboriginal people. In 1789 Alexander Mackenzie followed a gigantic river (now called the Mackenzie) to its mouth at the Beaufort Sea. Between 1819 and 1847 Sir John Franklin led three expeditions to map the coastline and search for the Northwest Passage.

ALEXANDER MACKENZIE

Above the Arctic Circle lies the land of the midnight sun. In June there are 24 hours of sunlight. In December there are no hours of light — the sun never rises.

The northern lights (aurora borealis) are ribbons of coloured light that seem to dance in the night sky. Northern people have many myths to explain the lights.

Michael Kusugak of Rankin Inlet writes stories about his life as a child when his family travelled by dogsled across the sea ice. *Northern Lights: The Soccer Trails* tells an Inuit myth about the shimmering lights.

Singer/songwriter Susan Aglukark, from Arviat, is the first Inuit recording artist. She achieved a gold record (50 000 sold in Canada) with her fourth album, *This Child*.

1870

In 1870, after buying Rupert's Land from the Hudson's Bay Company and accepting the Northwest from Britain, Canada stretched to Alaska. In 1880, Britain also gave up the islands of the Arctic. To show ownership of this vast area the Canadian government established North-West Mounted Police detachments in such remote places as Pond Inlet and Aklavik.

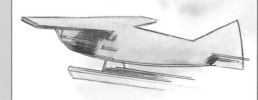

1905

In 1905 the 60th parallel of latitude was chosen as the southern boundary of the Territories. When minerals were found around Great Slave and Great Bear Lakes in the 1930s, settlers from the south moved in. Bush pilots flew miners and other workers into the area. Radio stations kept communities in touch. With the southerners came tuberculosis, influenza and other diseases, which killed many Aboriginal people.

1955

After World War II (1939–45) Americans felt nervous about a possible Russian attack over the North Pole. They wanted a string of radar stations across the North that would act as a warning system. The building of the Distant Early Warning System, or DEW Line, in 1955 brought in many workers.

TODAY

Modern technology is helping to develop the Territories' plentiful untapped mineral and oil deposits.

GLOSSARY

Canadian Shield
a rocky area covering 4.6 million km² (1.8 million sq. mi.) of Canada. From the air it looks like a shield surrounding Hudson Bay and stretching across the north to the Rocky Mountains. The Shield rock contains such minerals as gold, silver, copper, nickel, iron and zinc.

chart
a nautical (sailor's) map used at sea

Confederation
the uniting or joining together of three small British colonies to help themselves and one another. On July 1, 1867, the United Province of Canada (Canada East and Canada West), Nova Scotia and New Brunswick joined in a confederation. Each colony became a province of the new Dominion of Canada. Later more colonies joined the Confederation until Canada included the present ten provinces and two territories.

Continental Shelf
the seabed around the edges of a continent. It is covered by shallow water, usually no more than 100 fathoms (183 m [600 ft.]) deep, which makes it good for fishing.

erosion
the wearing away of land by the action of water or ice moving over the surface

fjord
a long, narrow bay. These steep-sided inlets along sea coasts are usually found in mountainous regions and are thought to have been dug out by glaciers sliding into the sea.

glacier
a mass of ice formed high in mountains by the pressure of deep snow. As the ice slides slowly down the mountains it begins to melt. The meltwater helps create rivers.

Great Depression
a period of hard times during which there was much unemployment worldwide. In 1928, farmers produced a huge crop of wheat, causing an oversupply. When the price of wheat fell suddenly, farmers couldn't afford to buy manufactured goods and factories had to close, putting many people out of work. The Great Depression lasted from 1929 to 1939.

inlet
a long, narrow passage that allows water to flow from a sea coast, riverbank or lakeshore into the land

latitude, parallels of
map lines drawn around the Earth parallel to the equator. They are numbered north and south from the equator, which is 0°. The 49th parallel of latitude north is used as the boundary between western Canada and the United States.

Loyalists
settlers who fled from the United States during the American Revolution (1775–83) because they wanted to live in British territory

muskeg
bog or wetland found in the northern areas of Canada. Mosses and black spruce grow in the spongy soil.

Northwest Passage
water route through the Arctic Islands. From the late 1400s many explorers searched for a northern route around North America because European countries wanted a fast route to China and India to trade for silks and spices. By the time Roald Amundsen of Norway found the passage in 1903, it was no longer needed.

pemmican
meat of the bison (plains buffalo) dried and ground into a powder, then mixed with animal fat and berries. It could be stored for many months.

permafrost
the short form for "permanently frozen ground," which is ground with a temperature that has stayed at or below 0°C (32°F) for at least two years. Permafrost covers nearly 50 per cent of Canada.

plateau
a large flat area of land, usually stretching between mountains. Some plateaus end in steep cliffs.

tipi
a cone-shaped tent made by covering a framework of poles with animal skins. These shelters were made by the Aboriginal people of the plains.